LEANDRO TAUB

The Hidden Mind

LEANDRO TAUB

LEANDRO TAUB

Leandro Taub is not a therapist, he's not a psychologist, he's not a doctor, he's not a coach, he's not a professional counselor and he isn't a guru. Leandro Taub dedicates himself to studying and shares through his books the results of his studies.

The success of Leandro Taub, the testimonials, and other examples used are exceptional and not typical, and do not pretend to be and will not guarantee that you or others will achieve the same results. Individual results will always vary depending on your own individual capacity, work ethic, abilities and experience, level of motivation, and other factors.

Leandro Taub's books, and Leandro Taub individually are not responsible for your actions. You are solely responsible for your own movements and decisions, and the evaluation and use of Leandro Taub's suggestions and ideas should be based on your own due diligence. You agree that Leandro Taub's books are not accountable to you in any way for their results in the use of his recommendations, the application of his writings in your life, and the interpretation you give to them.

Leandro Taub is in no way responsible for your actions, decisions, emotions and behaviors. Leandro Taub just offers his ideas. If you take Leandro Taub's ideas and decide to apply them in your life, it is absolutely and completely your responsibility and not Leandro Taub's.

As you read this book you agree to comply with and be bound by these conditions. If you are in opposition of any of these conditions, we suggest that you immediately cease the reading of this book and any other Leandro Taub's books. These Terms remain in effect and are effective as long as you are a reader of Leandro Taub books.

IF YOU DO NOT AGREE TO THESE TERMS, DO NOT READ THIS BOOK. BY READING THIS BOOK, YOU EXPRESSLY ACCEPT THESE TERMS, CONFIRM THAT YOU ARE AT LEAST 18 YEARS OLD AND HAVE THE LEGAL COMPETENCE TO PARTICIPATE IN A CONTRACT.

No material in this book may be copied, reproduced, republished, uploaded, published, transmitted, or distributed in any way without our express written permission. Violation of these terms may constitute an infringement of the copyright, trademark and other rights of TIKUN OLAM MEDIA and Leandro Taub. The contents of this book are protected by copyright, trade dress, and other state and federal laws, and may not be copied or imitated, in whole or in part.

Legal Warning
Leandro Taub, TIKUN OLAM MEDIA, and their affiliates do not assume any responsibility for any consequence related directly or indirectly to any action or inaction that you take based on the information that this book provides. While Leandro Taub strives to provide you with good, useful, and sound information, he cannot guarantee or assume responsibility for damages or losses related to the precision, integrity, or actuality of the information this book presents.

Except as specifically established in this document, to the maximum extent permitted in accordance with applicable law, Leandro Taub expressly refuses all warranties of any kind, whether express or implied, including, without limitation to, any warranty, suitable for one purpose in particular and non-infringing.

While Leandro Taub uses reasonable efforts to include correct and up-to-date information, Leandro Taub does not guarantee that the book will meet your requirements, or that the reading of the book will be free of errors. Leandro Taub offers no guarantees as to the results that may be obtained from the use of the book or of its content, accuracy, quality, or reliability of any information obtained through the book.

Limitations of Liabilities and damages
You accept the legal responsibility of Leandro Taub and TIKUN OLAM MEDIA including their responsibility of their affiliates, officials, directors, shareholders, employees or agents, for any claim made by you derived from the use of this book or from the use of the advice offered here. You agree that Leandro Taub is not a therapist, he is not a psychologist, he is not a doctor, he is not a coach, he is not a professional counselor, and he is not a guru, and he has no responsibility regarding your actions, or any consequences based on information or statements made by him in his books and digital media.

Under no circumstance will special, incidental, consequential or punitive damages be awarded, even if we have been advised of the possibility of such damages.

Compliance with the law
You agree to comply with all federal, state, and local laws, regulations, rules, and ordinances applicable to your use of this book.

Miscellaneous
You guarantee, declare and accept that, by reading this book, (i) you have carefully read and fully understand these Terms and fully understand its content, (ii) you are consenting to these Terms of your own free will, based on your own judgment and without any coercion or fear of retaliation, and (iii) you had the opportunity to consult independent legal counsel regarding these Terms.

THE HIDDEN MIND

First English Edition, August 2020

Book Cover Art and Interior Book Design: Leandro Taub

Copyright © 2020 TIKUN OLAM MEDIA

ISBN: 9781657647893

All rights reserved.

Under the penalties provided by law, is strictly prohibited without written permission of the copyright holders, the total or partial reproduction of this work by any means or process, including reprographics and informatics treatment as well as the distribution of copies by public rental or loan.

If you would like to receive news about the author, signup to his email list in www.leandrotaub.com

LEANDRO TAUB

DEDICATED TO DAD & MOM

THE HIDDEN MIND

LEANDRO TAUB

A COMMENT

This is a homemade translation so that my book, originally written in Spanish, reaches your language. It is possible that it has spelling errors, grammatical faults and lack of style. I deeply thank you for sending me any note or correction, so we can include it in the next edition of the book. Thank you.

studio@leandrotaub.com

THE HIDDEN MIND

LEANDRO TAUB

INDEX

	Acknowledgments	Pg 1
	Presentation	Pg 3
	Prologue	Pg 5
	Introduction	Pg 6
1	To Recognize	Pg 10
2	The Mind	Pg 29
3	Mental training	Pg 80
4	Opening the mind	Pg 104
5	Oneself and the world	Pg 112
6	Self-evaluation	Pg 129
7	Mental field	Pg 141
8	Mental healing	Pg 151
9	Beyond the mind	Pg 201
10	Surrender	Pg 212

THE HIDDEN MIND

LEANDRO TAUB

ACKNOWLEDGMENTS

Thanks to Alejandro Jodorowsky for his love, his service to humanity and the words he gave me for my book.

A special thank you to Fito Páez, for his friendship, example, and marvelous philosophical influence.

Thanks to Juan Aguado, Ezequiel Aizenberg, Luis Alfaro, Marco Álvarez, Pocho Álvarez, Fernando Barba, Emiliano Barbieri, Henry Barrial, Brian Gomes Bascoy, Niels Bent, Arthur Bizgu, María del Carmen, Sofía Gala Castiglione, Laura Cazares, Belén Chavanne, Rocío Crudo, Edu Arturo y Corazón Akáshico, Vale Durán, Ignacio Etchegoin, Camila Evia, Paula Fazio, Martín Fernandez, Matías Ferrié, Mariano Gold, Yeana Gonzáles, Iván Helman, Ariel Honigman, Pedro Kohn, Lidiya Korotko, Luciano Lasca, Joe Le Mat, Sofía Malamute, Gala Violeta Mansour, Negro Mariani, Brujito Maya, Sofía Medrano, Santiago Merea, Ana Milena Porras Marulanda, Álvaro Mizrahi, Maia Molina Carranza, Diana Mondino, Noe Mourier, Shanda de Nirvana, Alfredo Oliveri, Johanna Orrego, Natalia Oyanedel Issa, Berthnelly Pacheco Sosa, Margarita Páez, Martín Páez, Santiago Pando, Javier Páramo, Paola Casa OM, Mercedes Picco, Martín Prubner, Paula Reyes, Romina Richi, Francisco Roch, Marcos Rodríguez Alcobendas, Fernando Rubio, Carmen Sol, Vera Spinetta, Facu Taub, Mike Timm, Kathleen Truffaut, Lucía Trujillo, Steve Van de Geuchte, Salomé Vorfas, Natalia Yajia, Tamara Yajia y Jazmin Zang, for their presence in my life and accompanying me during the course of writing of this book.

Thanks to my life friends Guido Adler, Esteban Lubranecki, Ioni Rodgers, Matías Rosenberg.

Thanks to Marta Sevilla for accompanying me and being my ideal agent.

Eternally in me, thanks to Danna Luz Taub, Jonathan Taub, Emmanuel Taub, Mimi Feld and Julio Taub.

THE HIDDEN MIND

PRESENTATION

I asked Alejandro for a quote for the book's subtitle. The text he sent me deserves its own space, his page:

"The mind is what it is when it's empty of words. The heart is what it is when it's full of love. If the heart doesn't feel, the mind catalogs. If the heart is opened to others, the mind is silenced and compassion appears."

Alejandro Jodorowsky

THE HIDDEN MIND

PROLOGUE:

THE MIND

We are not our mind, but rather our mind is our main tool. If our essential being observes the mind, it will be able to recognize it, control it and train it. If our essential being identifies with our mind, it will not be able to observe it and it will not recognize it; it will believe that it *is* the mind and will get carried away by the primitive state that the mind finds itself in.

The mind gives form to matter. Our will carried out by thoughts, words, and deeds is the direct result of mental power. If we educate the mind, it will become our greatest ally. If we neglect it, it will become our greatest enemy. With an educated mind, we can choose objectives and directions. We can organize the present to advance in our search. With an uneducated mind, we dedicate ourselves to scrabbling, suspicion, limiting ourselves, generating stress, and suffering. It is possible to live with an educated mind. It does not depend on external factors, it comes down to the work towards the knowledge of ourselves.

The game I outline in this book is to believe that coincidences do not exist and that everything happens for a reason. Perhaps there isn't any isolated incident, instead everything functions as a constant *becoming*. If you accept these rules of the game as you read this book, there's a reason why you have it in your hands. It has something to tell you... or maybe it's you, through your mind, filtering what you receive to perceive what's useful to receive.

INTRODUCTION:

A TRUTH DISGUISED WITH ENDLESS LIES

Everything I am about to say is a lie. You can take it as a story, you can take it as fantasies, you can even take it if it's useful to you and dismiss it if it's not. As I write, I have no intention to be right; that's not what this is all about. The work I do is about research. May the unnamable save me from issuing any ephemeral truth from my mouth. I do not even consider myself capable of pronouncing a truth. That's why I will take what I consider the more useful road: lies.

This being said, I come to tell you that there aren't any rules on how to read this book, no set path is proposed nor any precise explanation you need to align with. I believe it is more convenient for you to let yourself be guided by your intuition and follow yourself; if your heart beats stronger at any part, if your emotions display any alterations, if you discover any kind of disturbance within you, then look again at what you just read. Maybe there, pinpointed by your own being, there is something that might prove useful to you. React to your own curiosity, it is the guide used by your depths to show you where to go. While working on this book, I did the same.

My aim in writing *The Hidden Mind* is to offer you the results I have so far found when exploring one of our most powerful tools: our mind. Along this path through the mind, I will offer a chance to analyze its secrets and ways. The intention is to provide something that can be of use. If the book accomplishes this objective, we have succeeded.

To achieve this aim, I propose you not to hold on to explanations or definitions. This objective cannot be achieved by imposition. One part in particular might be useful to some people and insignificant to others. Each person will realize as much, and not only realize it but also feel it, according to when they read the book, where they are, their present state (physical, sexual, emotional and intellectual), and the vital life experience they have stuck to their very skin the moment they read this book.

Do not take anything I say as an absolute truth, it cannot be. It's risky, being finite, to consider something as an infinite truth. The mind that hasn't yet dared to exit its comfort zone, challenging itself with training, normally, does this. This mind, by identifying itself with something that resonates, will take that as an absolute truth for as long as it identifies with it. Afterwards, if it succeeds in disassociating itself and has not trained in other aspects, it might end up feeling damaged, outraged, betrayed by that past reading and install a deception in its memory. Such a mind will not only do so with a text, it might also do so with relationships, work, family, laws, values, tastes and with so many other people, things, and circumstances. It will define something that it resonates with, take it as something set, and will project it toward eternity. This is why I tell you, and I do repeat, not to take anything I write as an absolute truth. Everything I say is finite (if not, I could not say it). Of the things I give, some have a weight and density that might make you think that they are set, that they are thus, a fact. Nevertheless, that is not so. Not even these are like this. Everything I write here is impermanent. Therefore, if you dare to delve into the reading of this book, I ask you not to respect any law and to go forward with care. Do not be careful with the words I say, but with yourselves instead. I feel a great responsibility in setting words to paper, writing to receptive eyes, with the risk of someone taking them as absolute and solidifying them within their life experience. For this reason, go ahead daring and with care! Take what is useful and as for the rest, leave them. And whatever you assimilate, do not let it be permanent; when it stops being useful, let it go.

Another important aspect is that you already know everything you're going to read. Maybe you remember some things, others maybe not. All the same, whether you remember it or not, you already know. Everything I possibly have access to; you also already have. The mystery existing within your depths, that coexists with you belonging to a 'where' without 'where' and a 'when' without 'when' (beyond time and space), can access all manifested knowledge. The material with which I work while I write is one that I hear, that reaches me from these very depths that reside in everyone. They are the sparks of creation, appearing in ancient books as the flames of supreme wisdom. Working on these sparks has helped me discover that everything is here, and everything exists. All that *was*, *is* and *will be* is among us. If it's not here, it never was nor will be. Thoughts do not stop echoing in the universe. From the first manifested thought in the cosmos to the last, they are all at our disposal. These sparks are happening around us all the time. Telepathy exists and is our real way of communication, the one we use not only to communicate between us, but also to channel the sparks occurring around us. We function like radio antennas. I don't want to complicate the issue yet, it's only the beginning. However, I believe it is useful to write it, to capture part of the roadmap I will use as I compose this book.

There is a spark of creation coming from the essence, it descends and is chained through certain worlds for us to be here, we take a body and give form to it. This spark brings about all the laws through which we are created. We are made with the same laws that produced the universe, through sparks of creation. If we come to know ourselves, we will be able to know these sparks. Knowing this, we will be able to know the universe. This said, if we come to know ourselves, we can come to know the entire universe. It is all here, contained within us. It is all here within.

There is not a franchise in the universe, where some are inscribed, among other prophets, having the capacity to channel these sparks and own them (the world understands and feels what one of them said thousands of years ago and thinks it was him, whilst what he did was just channel a piece of knowledge available to everything existing in the universe). Therefore, it does not concern some being able to access this wisdom and not others. These sparks circulate among us. Everyone can channel them. If someone simply sees the spark and does nothing about it, they will later forget it. One can be taking a shower when an answer reaches them, they feel it, but do nothing with it; they move on and then forget it. If someone takes the spark, something begins to happen.

My work, what I dedicate myself to, is to capture these sparks. I channel them through letters, words, and actions. I usually carry small notebooks where I write down everything that comes to me. From this, I begin to organize them and they transform into my maps of action in the world. This has to do with taking sparks and delivering them. This is what I dedicate myself to. Therefore, nothing that you are going to read in this book is of my complete authorship. It would be vane on my part to write something believing that I have made it. There is a story behind me and another ahead of me. The entire universe dictates me through these sparks. This is how one becomes a bridge; the essence works through those who do not resist. And this very work will be the one that guarantees that everything I write here will be a lie. It will be so because I am not the one who dictates the spark. This will not arrive cleanly to you, through me, but it is translated through the languages I have been programmed with and is being passed through the filter of vital experiences I have had these years. Therefore nothing I say can be an absolute truth. At most, achieving the objective that I am proposing, my words will be able to act as useful lies, hiding an indescribable truth that can only be felt and never translated. This will also imply that I do not have the capacity to do something new, I am not creating something as I write these lines.

Let us close the introduction and get to work. Remember: nothing I say is new, you already know all of this. I do not have the capacity to create anything (only to take sparks and to transmit them through my vital experience). I come here to lie to you, everything I have said and everything I will say is a lie: do not assimilate anything as an absolute truth (at most, if it is useful take it and if it is not useful leave it, at any rate these are lies). Finally, welcome to The Hidden Mind, a book of fables and lunacy to recognize the mind, control it, train it, and come to know ourselves.

CHAPTER 1

RECOGNIZING

1. MEMORY OF DEATH
2. THE SILENCE OF THE WISE
3. WITH MIND AND HEART
4. THE FOUR CENTERS
5. PERFECT ASYMMETRY
6. CH-CH-CH-CH-CHANGES

1. MEMORY OF DEATH

Let us begin with the first lie that I will tell you in this book: we are all going to die. I will die, you will die; we will die, the people we know will die, the ones we used to know will die, the ones we will know will die; everyone who has been and will be born will die. Let us not get into the topics of conscience, of mind, of emotion; nothing that can be beyond the body. Let us begin with the most simple and basic: we are living through a body that has been born, is living and will die. This is one of the fundamental laws of this manifestation and no one can abandon it: to be able to live, one must be born and die.

But what if I am not just a body?

If I am not just a body, and am instead living and experiencing life through this body (which was born and will die), then everything I have written before changes. I will not die, you will not die, we will not die, the ones we used to know, those we know and those we will know will not die. Now I will write it like this: the body through which I live is going to die, the body through which you live is going to die, the bodies with which everyone we knew, know and will know live through, are going to die.

But why are you telling me this?

Because more than one person lives without remembering this. The bodies through which we experience this life are going to die. Can we remember this? I ask because more than one person will identify with what they are reading now, but in a few minutes they will forget it again. It is useful to remember it over and over again: you, me, everyone we knew, know and will know, have a finite amount of time in the bodies they live in. And all this about not remembering seems simple, but it gets more complicated: not only do we not remember that the body through which we experience life will die, but many also do not remember themselves.

But who is 'oneself'?

A few months ago, someone asked me: "What do I do to forget about it?", and I answered: "You forget it the same way you forgot how you felt on May 5th at 9:25 pm". If I were to ask you what you were feeling on the 7th of October 2011 at 8:03 pm, would you remember it? You have no idea, you would not know what to answer (surely, it would be pleasant if some day someone was to tell me that they remember). While we are living here, we don't remember what has happened, much less remember ourselves (and if you do remember something, it is far from what actually happened, and more like an artificiality translated from a neurotic fantasy and projective based on a memory housed in the subconscious). Nevertheless, at the moment that this feeling is present, we identify ourselves absolutely and completely with it, to the point where we believe that it is our eternity. Evaluate yourselves. You will find that when you identify with an emotion, you believe that it will last forever. You project that emotion onto your whole life. You identify yourself with a fight, a pain, an envy, falling in love, a challenge (or "problem", according to some people) and you project it onto your whole life. You completely identify with this emotion the moment it occurs and, paradoxically, the very next moment you take on a new thought that translates into feelings, you identify yourself with this one and forget all about the former. There are also opposing cases: the body has already changed, but the mind remains attached and clings to something that happened. Then, a disruption is generated: the body wants to advance, the emotions are willing to flow, however, the mind (uncontrolled) is forcing the situation, introducing the neurotic memory to keep the feeling that it does not want to let present go. This is exactly where problems begin.

I want to reconnect you to the urgency of the present, bring you here, where everything is happening. Thus, I am going to return to something I said at the beginning: the body through which you are experiencing life is going to die. What do you feel when I tell you this? It sounds grim, maybe tormenting, a little insensitive, rather demented, a bit crazy… or it sounds evident, obvious, simplistic, easy. There are many possible definitions you can give it.

Now, I want you to distance yourself from the definition for the time being, forget about putting a name to things and read me carefully: the body through which you are experiencing life is going to die. For years you have lived pretending it isn't so, you have put a veil over your eyes, some kind of transparent layer that instils in you a false sense of tranquility and takes you away from that terrible weight of knowing that the body through which you are experiencing life is going to die. You knew since you were a child. You woke up in the middle of the night screaming, calling your mother and your father, asking for an answer, the immense emptiness of recognizing the existence of death tormented you; you introduced yourself into that void where it all ends, where there are no more games, no more adventure, no more growth, no more learning, no more leisure, no more desire, no more ideas, no more creation.

But mum, dad, am I going to die? Are you going to die? Are we all going to disappear? My brothers and sisters also? Will there be nothing else?

Do you remember this? It was a tremendous moment of emptiness. You realized that you were living in a movie that had an end and that end included you: you were going to disappear in the form you were in. And yet the impact was intensified: you recognized that not just the body through which you experience life was going to die, but also that of your father and mother, that of your brothers and sisters, that of your grandfathers and grandmothers, that of your friends, that of your colleagues, and why not, also that of your sons and daughters.

You know, but you do not know. You know, but you live as if you do not. You know it but you do not remember it. You know it, but you ignore it. You know it, but you do not pay much attention to it. You know it, but you lie to yourself. Then, by pulling a veil over death, you live as if eternity might resolve what you are not resolving. For example, you allow yourself to do things you do not like, because of a longing for the future, believing that life is eternal and that at some point, you will change activity. For example, you allow yourself to be with people that do you no good, because of a longing for the future, believing that the situation will adjust itself. For example, you allow yourself not to follow your dreams, believing that at some point in the future, your possibility will magically arrive. For example, you allow yourself to live a life that is not yours, because you believe yourself to be a victim of a divine order, because you believe that you cannot fulfill your dreams, because if you believe it, you will not know how and you become lost in despair and suffering. Living as though eternity would solve what you don't allow all of this.

But what happened? At some moment you forgot this. Perhaps you remember it for a time, when someone you have an emotional bond with dies. Then you remember and later, you forget it again. That veil that you have drawn to separate yourself from death also separates you from a part of yourself. How many times do you remember the existence of death daily? Weekly? Monthly? Yearly? Paradoxically, you would not be able to live if death did not exist. When you live without remembering death, you forget the urgency, life loses that ever heavy vertigo of the ephemeral, of the finite. The memory of what we have is time, and just for a while, because it goes away. There is a stopwatch running backwards and it is going to stop.

If you remember death, if you bring that existential void to the present, life can take a more powerful, urgent facet than usual; one that will never make you do something that you don't want to again; no more harmful relationships, no more jobs that you don't enjoy, no more studies that are not guided by your curiosity, no more saying something that doesn't represent you, no more activities that don't fill you with pleasure and joy, no more things you don't want, never another second spent on something you don't choose with all your being. Listen to the call of death. It can happen today, tomorrow, within two days, within a year, within a hundred years: it is imminent and unpredictable.

The body through which you are experiencing life is going to die. Feel it. I do not say this to you to make you fall into despair, neither to make you suffer. I say it to bring you to the present. Feel it and come back to your present, knowing that life is long, yet not so much. Feel it and make your life useful, say goodbye to the useless. Live. You are worthy, you are deserving, if you want it, you can; it is possible and it depends on you.

You cannot avoid death, what you can do is choose what you do while you live here. You can decide how and how long you live. You can influence your physical, sexual, emotional, and mental health while you are here. The longevity of life you experience depends on you. And your evolution depends on your work with yourself.

If the life you experience has an end date, do you want to waste time from your life? You have been given a finite amount of time here, to do some work, to discover yourself, to set objectives for yourself and to achieve them. Ask yourself, how useful can it be to waste a certain present for an uncertain future? I say this because many live at that level, they sacrifice a great part of their lives to have a materially prosperous grave. Bear in mind that level of urgency; the one that compels you to come here, to the present. It is very powerful. Stop forgetting death, perhaps, and maybe you will cease to forget yourself.

If we do not know what comes after death, it is for a reason. We live and experience life through a body that works as a process in constant change, from the moment it is born until the moment it dies. We do not know (or we do not remember) what is before life, nor what comes after. The antithesis of death is not life, but birth. They both function as bridges. Birth as a bridge from the unknown toward life. Death as a bridge from life toward the unknown. What is in between is what we live.

2. THE SILENCE OF THE WISE

Humility is the first and fundamental quality of wisdom. A wise person is in a constant process of learning. You might find them in conversation; they are not the one presenting their ideas, they are instead the silent one, the one who listens and learns, the one who listens to what is happening. Without humility, there is no possible entrance. Humility is what allows you to listen. A person who is entertained by talking and expounding on an idea, for that moment, is not giving themselves the space for what is new. Those who listen in silence, open possibilities and their capacity to absorb.

This book that you are reading is not a single book; it is as many books as the times it is read. Everyone that reads it will do so distinctly, they will take from it according to their vital experience and what their mental body allows them to absorb. This is so because the mind performs as a filter; according to how it resonates with every part of the reading, it will project what the essential being needs to see at every moment. This being so, what each person reads is what each person wants and should read. And not only that; if the same person reads the book more than once, they will discover that it is not the same book. The process status has changed, the body is already different, the mind is different, the emotions and sexuality have changed and the experience of the essential being for this incarnation has also mutated. If two people, having read the same book, meet, they might pretend that they agree about certain parts they have read. They might fake that they agree on some things; that, however, would not be true. Each of them has read a completely different book; each of them experienced what they had to through what was read.

The truth is one, the essence is the same. The absolute from which we come is within all space and within all time. We can take the sparks of creation, capture a few answers from this supreme wisdom running through all of us, and its capturing will be the same for all. However, as we lower it, pass it through the mental filter to organize it and shape it, by whatever means, we are perverting it, giving it the ink of life experience lived by our essential being in this world. Then it ceases to be the pure truth, and becomes one of the infinite interpretations that can be given to something, without necessarily coinciding between what some say it is and what others say it is.

A person who has not worked on training their mind, who has not given it space yet, will believe that their interpretation of the truth is the same for everyone. That their vision is the same as that of others; and will project their experience as the very truth. A person who has not worked on training their mind will not discover the humility of the wise; avoiding silence, they will look to expound on their own point of view, their opinion, their speech. They will attempt to demonstrate something and assure themselves that everyone agrees. They will interrupt others to display what they know, clinging to that small previously acquired knowledge and not offering themself the capacity to discover something new, to incorporate new knowledge.

A person who trains their mind discovers the great benefits of silence and listening, of learning constantly from all. A person who trains their mind may come to ask themself before speaking: is what I want to say useful or useless? Can it offer anything to anyone? Is it helpful? Does it provide anything or is it just exteriorized vanity? A person who trains their mind is going to measure what they think, say, and do, and will listen to as much as they can, cancelling their experienced knowledge and in doing so, giving themself enough space for new input; and once having acquired the new knowledge, will eliminate it again for new input, and so on successively.

3. WITH MIND AND HEART

What we can see, we capture through the mind, and what we feel and experience can be so when passed through the heart. Our advancement and evolution depends on the dialogue between these two.

One affair is understanding something and another is to feel it. When we think, we can understand. When we feel, we can be. When we think, we can understand why we do what we do. When we feel, we can *do*. An individual who understands but does not feel knows what to do but is not able to do so. A person who feels but does not understand is able to *do* but does not understand. It is for this reason that the work to be done is double, from the mind– our fundamental and most powerful tool that guides our experience through life – to follow through the heart – which feels and has the capacity to bring intellectual awareness to the flesh, which makes what is thought be lived and determines what we do and what we don't--. Believing it and knowing it are not the same. When we believe it, it is just in our thoughts, in an intellectual activity. Once we know it, we have already felt it. Once we understand and realize it, we can know it. And once we know it, it is not necessary to believe it anymore, now we know it.

Attention is what translates the mind to the heart. When we pay attention, the mind focuses on the object of our attention. The emotional body then points in that direction, following the mind, and will begin to feel. Once the mental and emotional body meet at the object of observation, learning begins.

4. THE FOUR CENTERS

The minor arcana of the tarot can be separated into four suits. These four suits correspond to the four points of the cross that composes the human being. At the masculine sky hemisphere, the sword. At the feminine sky hemisphere, the cups. At the masculine earth hemisphere, the wands. At the feminine earth hemisphere, the pentacles. The swords correspond to the eagle, a carnivorous animal, essentially active, acting from the sky plane and represents the element of air. The cups correspond to the angel, a vegetarian being, essentially passive, which receives from the sky plane and represents the element of water. The wands correspond to the lion, a carnivorous animal, essentially active, acting from the earth plane and represents the element of fire. The pentacles correspond to the ox, a vegetarian animal, essentially passive, receiving from the earth plane and represents the element of earth.

The center associated with the sword is intellect which, like a sword, must be forged, tempered, and sharpened to become an excellent sword; intellect must be recognized, worked on and trained to become a great tool. The center associated with the cups is the heart which, like these, receive, accumulate, and deliver liquids, being able to be decorated in their labor; the heart receives, accumulates, and delivers emotions, being able to be worked on in its gift of loving. The center associated with the wands is sex which, like these, sprout and grow naturally from the earth, working instinctively and associated with the animal kingdom; sexuality sprouts and grows naturally from desire, working through the most primitive and instinctive part of the being and is linked to its animality. The center associated with the pentacles is the body which, like gold extracted from the earth, is struck, worked on, and finally, delivered back to earth; the body comes from the dust and to the dust it returns. We receive it from mother earth, we form it, we give it health, and finally, it returns to mother earth.

Intellect belongs to the sky plane; it is essentially active; it is represented by air, the swords and the eagle; its universe is that of thoughts and it must be forged, tempered and sharpened to become great intellect. The heart belongs to the sky plane; it is essentially receptive; it is represented by water, the cups, and the angel; its universe is that of emotions and its function is receiving, accumulating, and delivering emotions. In this give and take, it must flow in order not to perish. Sex belongs to the earth plane; it is essentially active; it is represented by fire, the wands, and the lion; its universe is that of desires and it works through the most instinctive and primitive. In order to achieve its realization, the desire must be concentrated. The body belongs to the earth plane; it is essentially receptive; it is represented by earth, the pentacles, and the ox; its universe is that of the needs and it is received from the earth. It works on itself by offering health through breathing, nutrition, movement, sleep, and thoughts and its destiny is to inevitably return to the earth.

There is an intelligence present in each of these four centers: intellectual intelligence, emotional intelligence, sexual intelligence, and physical or mechanical intelligence. Each one can be trained by the mind and affected by the others and therefore, for its proper performance, it must work independently from these. The intervention from one onto the other happens to complement, correct, or alter. Once programmed, each intelligence works very well on its own. Nevertheless, they are all a part of the essential being, they are guided by themselves and must keep changing and developing constantly to evolve into the manifestation and not transform into obstacles. At every moment the four intelligences are working simultaneously, each of them doing what it must for the performance of the whole vehicle that composes us. They come to be our four wheels; they can all point toward the same place and the vehicle moves in that direction, just as they can each point toward a different direction and the vehicle wont advance. The movement of one affects the others. It is independent in its ability to perform and dependent in its constant interaction and influence with the other intelligences.

Sit down and put your hands under your buttocks, in a way that they are trapped and you cannot move your fingers. Close your eyes and imagine a keyboard and your hands in front of it. Now try to write a phrase on the imaginary keyboard. See how long it takes you to write the phrase. Or get into the car you drive and instead of doing it automatically, try to set your thoughts and decide intellectually when to step on the clutch, when on the brake, when to look through the rearview mirror, etc. Or try to emit every word while paying attention to each of the letters and how you say them. Or try not to read this text automatically, instead pay attention to each of the words, reading them completely. In all cases the same occurs: lag. If you want to write on a keyboard using intellect, the writing process is slowed. If you want to drive a car using intellect towards the decisions, your reaction capacity is slowed and you drive brutally. This happens because you are involving another intelligence—intellectual— to do the work of another that has already been programmed to do it and knows how— in this case, physical intelligence. If you program physical intelligence, it will know how to perform on its own, automatically, facing the situations requiring its program. Observe how you do it daily. You have the walking program (if the program was taken away, you would not be able to maintain equilibrium nor walk), you have the speech and reading program (if they would take away the program, you would not be able to speak or read), you have the program to write on a keyboard, to drive a car, or play piano. These are some examples of the numerous programs incorporated into the physical intelligence we have to act. On its own, the program is very well executed. When interfered with by one of the other intelligences, it is disturbed and the physical program does not work properly. Nevertheless, the physical program started with the mind. The mind programmed the body initially, it gave the order to start a practice and after repetition during a certain period, the physical intelligence succeeded in absorbing the new knowledge and bringing it to its programming. It was at this point that the intellect's intervention proved useful for programming. Then, it allowed the physical intelligence to work on its own. If a new program must be introduced, the intervention of another intelligence will be necessary again; for example, if we want to incorporate a new language to the ones we have already assimilated. In the case of wanting to correct some part of one of the programs, for instance, wanting to improve one of the already added languages, then, there is once again an intervention of one of the other intelligences; the mind investigates concerning the new language and the order to practice is sent, carrying out a daily exercise of new words, the grammar, the pronunciation, and the style of that language, introducing this improvement into the physical program. Physical intelligence is programmed and improved through practice. A great musician, a great painter, a great athlete, a great laborer, a great pilot, a great mechanic, a great electrician; the excellence levels discovered within some physical activities were achieved through practice, programming the physical intelligence, and improving it continuously.

Try to perform a sexual act while thinking about where to put each arm, how you position your hip, the tones at which you groan, what to say and what not to, how you grasp, how tight to hold on, etc. What will happen is that you will not be able to get to climax. Try to come up with a story while thinking about what the outcome will be and how you will write each sentence. What will happen is that you will not be able to create the story. Sexual intelligence is related to the most instinctive, primitive, and natural part of our being. This intelligence is neither planned nor intervened; if you want to think and plan it, nothing happens. For sexual intelligence to arrive at its climax in the sexual act or for the sexual act to be performed in full freedom and creativity
, you must allow it to act by itself. Sexual intelligence, acting by itself, is working from the most primitive nature where there is no planning nor thought, just being and feeling. If the intellect is silenced and does not analyze, if the physical program does not act, but instead *is*, the body will be present and be able to feel. As you feel, the creative sexual act surges spontaneously. As you feel, the sexual intelligence will work efficiently. If the desire is concentrated (placing the focus of attention on what is being done, in the present situation), sexual intelligence will achieve the climax and be able to create. What needs to work here is the instinctive and primitive side, our animality, our sexual and creative force. Intellect cannot replace desire. If you establish another center, you will not be able to be there to fulfill the desire. Intellect can decide where to concentrate our desire, where we place the focus of our attention, then a full presence is needed for the sexual center to work on its own.

Try to analyze a loving relationship with intellect. What you give, what you receive, how you give it, how you receive it, how you speak to each other, what you say, when you say it, what you feel, how you feel it, etc. You will discover that you can sketch out major theories about emotional relationships, you can learn a lot about your emotions however, you cannot share, open yourself to shared emotions and loving exchanges. Emotional intelligence works on its own and when intervened with by other centers, it is interrupted and does not know how to act, it intrudes into enigmas and emotional dilemmas, it hinders itself and does not experience. If left to work by itself, emotional intelligence will share by its nature and gift of giving, it will open to relate and will be intuitive in its behavior. It will act by emotion and not by analysis. In the case where a repeated emotion or an emotional blockage arises, the intervention of another intelligence will be useful indeed to unlock or review the reason for repetition. If something is confusing within the emotional center and the heart is not offering itself freely, there may be a restrictive idea lodged in the subconscious; intellect acts without our attention, and maybe it is not allowing the heart to carry out its gift in action, giving and sharing with humility and freedom. Emotional life does not pass through reasoning, nor through logic, nor through sex, nor through the body; it passes through itself. Emotional life lives at its peak if emotions are not suppressed and are permitted to flow with their nature, that they may expand and contract, may the cup be filled and given to drink, over and over, within a constant gift of sharing. Emotional relationships function like an exchange, like the heart itself. Heartbeats are double, as the heart beats it gives and receives blood. An emotional center that is healthy and fully functioning is double: as it beats, it gives and receives. From the emotional, it shares.

The intellectual center is the captain of the ship: it has greater influence over the other centers, it has the capacity to train them, alter them, change their focus of attention, or allow them to be. This center can be silent, receptive, or active. In turn, by being receptive or active, it can do it positively, negatively, or neutrally. According to where the mode of action finds itself and where the focus of attention is placed, the other centers will follow. If any of the other centers is not functioning freely, the intellectual center is the one that can intervene to assist.

All intelligences should be circulating for the health of the being to be complete. If they are blocked, it is because, at a mental level, it was decided to be so; some thought, word, or physical action is being made against that center, an idea was deposited that is restricting it, or an astral blockage was developed that does not allow it to be.

The mind is marvelous for getting us where we want to go. The mind is fabulous for defining objectives, directions, and organizing. It also works very well for entering other centers and training or unlock them. However, an uncontrolled mind is capable of blocking the centers, stunning them, modifying them, not allowing their free circulation, their experiences, and adequate living.

There is a physical intelligence that works very well. If we interpose it with intellectual intelligence it will slow down. If we program it, it will work very well by itself later on. It will be useful to involve intellect for reprogramming it, improving it, and then releasing it to let it be on its own. There is a sexual intelligence that has its own intelligence and knows very well to do its job, by performing from the instinctive. If we interrupt it and add intellect, it blurs. If we leave it be, it works very well. There is an emotional intelligence that functions very well by itself, that acts from the emotional and naturally shares and opens itself to live. If we include intellectual intelligence there, it will ruin things.

There are several intelligences working simultaneously within the body. The best we can do with each one is to let it be. Let each part do its job. It is useful to involve and mix them to educate, unblock, and calm; it is useful when there is something that is addicted or at an extreme: if the heart leads you to emotional jealousy, attachment, envy in excess, the intelligence will be useful there because it can reeducate emotions, educate the heart. If the body does not understand how to drive a car, it is not about throwing yourself away, it is about calling the mind to educate the body: start the engine, then
the gear, the clutch, the brake... The body should be educated by the mind until it works alone and then the mind will leave and let the body be and act on its own. The same applies for sex and creativity. Then, it is good to mix the centers when necessary for educating or unblocking, and when not, let them be. Each center has its own program, its own intelligence, and fulfillment situation. They work very well on their own. If we want to replace one with another, problems arise. It is useful for the mind to intervene when there is something to assist: helping to unblock if there is anything blocked, helping to educate if there is anything to exercise. It is not useful if we pretend to replace instead of exercise.

So, I began with the mind, the starting point. It is the last border between separation and unity, between our characters and our essential being, between the embodied soul and the divine soul, between manifestation and the manifested. It begins with the perception realized by the mind. The centers are trained from the mind and the silenced mind allows them to be. The centers are blocked by the mind and the mind, triggering, affects them. The centers are unblocked by the mind and the mind that trains itself improves them.

5. PERFECT ASYMMETRY

Some have a rigid and static image of perfection, unchangeable for being at its maximum point of expression. Something rigid, something permanent, is not possible in life because life itself passes; manifestation is in change, like an impermanent process, in constant transformation.

But there is another perfection: a dynamic, connected to the sacred of our passage through this manifestation. A perfect heart is not a hard one, but one filled with love and always ready to give. The mind that reaches perfection is one that uses concentration and returns to a mental state of annihilation, a meditative state. Sexuality working at levels of perfection concentrates its wishes in one direction, channeling, fulfilling, and invading the space with its act. A body working at a level of perfection is one that does not repress itself in any field and is in full flow, allowing itself to occupy all environments, broadening itself, without repressing its flow. These types of perfections are not something static, they are instead levels of excellence that keep transforming.

A person who falls into the pursuit of perfectionism attempts to attain an impossible position, because it can *always* be improved. Attempt to solidify something that cannot be solidified. Try to reach a level of perfection that cannot be achieved in manifested form. Whoever recognizes the changing nature of things can point to excellence levels and allow themselves to further progress.

The mind that continues to train works to reach excellence, knowing that at some moment it should conclude and renounce because it cannot reach absolute perfection while everything it does changes. It knows that the castle it is building will be destroyed, that nothing it does will remain.

We come into the world imperfect and of asymmetrical form: we have one eye larger than the other, one breast bigger than the other, one testicle lower than the other, one hand larger than the other, all asymmetric. Because we are manifested, dynamically. Life, so beautiful and intelligent – did not make us symmetrical. If we were symmetrical we would not advance. Perhaps in that case, we could be perfect. Being imperfect, we are asymmetrical, and it becomes possible to make life dynamic.

We are asymmetric, life is asymmetrical, and this is what allows us to move from stability to instability, what allows us to move on. Without instability, we do not advance. We would not be able to live. There would not be time. In order for time to exist, asymmetry is necessary; if not, unity cannot be extended, everything remains compressed into one thing - our closest root. And there, there is no time. Time only arises with duality (dynamic, imperfect, polarities). And there cannot be space because it arises with the third (creation, maintenance, destruction, the three necessary rules for something to manifest). Even so, man cannot exist because the fourth is necessary to be born (the emergence of Tao, the impersonal force, the neutral, what is there after the being, not being, and the result of that being). One: essence; two: time; three: space and nature manifested at a wild level; Four: the man arises, the meeting of the four elements. With the fifth, man goes beyond himself, it is the crisis that takes him from stability to commence his astral journey.

6. CH-CH-CH-CH-CHANGES

Everything changes, everything passes, nothing remains, everything transforms. An implicit rule of manifestation is that it is in constant motion and permanent progress. Everything that manifests, everything that appears in this world, from the smallest cells to the most massive galaxies, all follow the cycles of birth, growth, transformation, decline, and death. Nothing can be rigid. Nothing can be constant. If it came into this universe, it is because it was born, and if it was born, it will die. If it came into this universe, it would advance from transformation to transformation, as an ongoing process that does not stop. And so it is for the planets, for the trees, for the buildings, for the stars, for human beings, for emotions, thoughts, for everything that *is*. We do not know our true identity, we do not know who we are, if we can see through what we live. The body we live through functions as a constant process, changing all the time, from moment to moment. The habits and customs with which we define ourselves are not fixed, they function in perpetual transformation and if the essential being is disguised as a healthy person, this process won't stop, but it will be in constant mutation; it won't cling to habits and customs but will instead change them according to the requirements of each situation. The activities we define ourselves with are not set, they come and go towards something, always changing. Everything built with the four elements, everything around us that can be made out of earth, fire, water, and air, do not belong to us, they are impermanent: they are temporary and ephemeral, always changing. Our essence, our essential being, our root, what belongs to us, can be beyond this changing matter. However, it does not appear and we do not see it, we cannot perceive it, it is what motivates us without us knowing it is there, what drives us even though we do not recognize it. All formed construction, all performed works, are ephemeral. Their times change and so does the speed of those changes. Everything changes and everything passes. Everything that has risen will fall. Everything that was built will be destroyed. Everything that was born will die.

When becoming aware of the ephemeral nature of things, the benefit of contradiction appears. There is no affirmation that can last for an exceptionally long time, at a certain moment, it will fall by its own weight. Each true value will become untrue at some moment. Each definition taken will lose its value. What rules will stop ruling. Everything is in constant change. And those who dare to adopt the change progress with the world. Those who dare to live with the change live with the world. Those who dare to develop their powers, to know, to dare, and to do will be able to progress and live in the world, without necessarily being from the world. Those who do not pay attention to the changes, who resist changes, who cling to definitions and identify themselves with what happened are covered by the world's changes. It is like a wave: who sees it and dares, can choose how to position the body and how to act with the wave's presence, whoever pays attention and dares, can take it and progress with the wave, whoever pays attention and does not dare can pass the wave without great results, and whoever does not see it is covered and dragged by it. There are no good and bad movements, there are no good and bad changes. Any change is an opportunity, and as everything is change, we live in a land of full opportunity. Becoming exasperated or suffering is an option, not an obligation. It is for those who do not dare to live with the changes and progress with them. A full life can be lived, of happiness, joy, and development, progressing and changing, allowing us to constantly transform.

The health of the vehicle with which we experience this life, of our body, of our sexuality, of the heart, and of our mind, depend on circulation. This circulation is the one advancing constantly with the changes. The lack of health of any of our bodies happens when we are missing that circulation; when we obstruct it, block it, repress it, or forbid it. When what is generated is illness, a new change arises. Even being able to generate the death of our vehicle (body), another change is generated. To those who do not allow change, life forces them to change. Death is a form of change for the body that no longer has any more space to make another vital change.

The essential being knows what it is doing and does not necessarily know our disguises. It lives and experiences through the manifested in constant transformation. However, it experiences life through the mind, and from the mind it experiences the intellectual, emotional, sexual, and physical body. If the mind is not allowed to change with life, if the mind keeps clinging on to something, if the mind deposits restrictive ideas, we do not remove health from our essential being, but from our character, from the person through whom we live. As we do not allow the person to change, forms of discomfort begin to be generated. Because something that wants to change is not doing it, or because something that is changing is doing so with obstacles. The bodies integrating us will seek by any means to go ahead with the constant process of change. It is unavoidable for them to do so and they do it. If the resistance is large, that which does not allow change is what forces death to act as a form of change.

Those who learn to govern their vehicle, control their mind, train their heart, sexuality, and body, will then be able to allow themselves to constantly change together with life. They will perhaps even be able to develop a will so great that they will be capable of choosing and doing, without being carried away by the events that cross them.

CHAPTER 2

THE MIND

1. THE POWER OF THE MIND
2. HOW WE TAKE IT, WE LIVE IT
3. UTILITIES OF THE MIND
4. RISKS OF THE MIND
5. PARTS OF THE MIND
6. THE UNSTABLE MIND
7. THE INTELLECT
8. THE SUBCONSCIOUS
9. THE EGO
10. SUMMARY OF THE PARTS OF THE

MIND AND ACTIVITIES TO BE DONE BY EACH

11. WAYS OF ACTING

12. MENTAL AGITATION

13. MENTAL DISPERSION

14. GATHERING MENTAL WAVES

15. CONCENTRATION

16. MENTAL ANNIHILATION

17. CONTROLLED AND UNCONTROLLED MIND

18. WORK TO DO

19. EXAMPLES

1. THE POWER OF THE MIND

Although we are not seeing it, because we do not see thoughts, the mind generates karma. It sends orders to the universe, and that comes back. So, an uncontrolled mind attracts what it needs and attracts obstacles whilst progressing. An educated mind will know, with much care, how to use its powers and will do so with full attention.

Karma is the law of action and attraction. This means that any performed action generates a reaction. If with one hand you move an object that is next to you at this moment, the movement done with your hand is the action and the movement of the object is the reaction. Karma is what is behind the well-known phrase "you reap what you sow". Karma is the web of causality that will justify that coincidences do not exist as such. To the human being who is programmed for today's world, built under false superstitions and crazy programs, coincidences exist. And they do not just exist, they rule their lives; they are translated as accidents, luck, bad luck, and other similar phenomena. To the human being who has disconnected themself a little from that program, who has allowed themself to look a little further, coincidences stop having such rigor and pass to become the result of what they do.

Karma for the Orient, the law of cause and effect for the Occident, or the soul's clothes for the cabala – they are called clothes because the soul uses this dress, it can be put on or taken off by taste and choice-. These are the thinking, the word, and the physical action. This means that everything you think, everything you say, and everything you do generate a reaction within the universe. These three forms of acting we have work as mandates that we send to the universe.

And everything comes back. It comes back like a boomerang that comes back to whom threw it, but not necessarily by the same way it was delivered. This is what is behind another known phrase: "Do not do unto others what you would not want done to yourself".

The bigger the work on yourself, the more you will dominate your thoughts, words, and deeds. The bigger your authority over them, the less "coincidences" will exist in your life. You will pass to see everything as a web of connected causalities, where everything that happens to you is a constant becoming of the relationship you have with the world through your deeds.

Therefore, it is of great importance to observe the way we think, talk, and act in the world. If we can observe, we will see the mandates we are launching. We are generating many things in these three levels.

It is an endeavor. It is not about you reading this, understanding it, and after that, dominating it perfectly. No, you are quite far from this. However, you can get closer. You will realize that it is a work and discipline of much rigor. The key tool is the mind's education and self-observation.

It is, perhaps, and only perhaps, that this work of self-observation goes against nature; it may reach to be that perhaps even evolution itself goes against nature. They strive to advise that it is good to go with the river, that you allow yourself to flow, but fish do not always swim with the current: sometimes they do and sometimes they do not, they have a will they can manage. Which are the only fish that always swim with the current? Dead fish. Maybe, and just maybe, when we say "flow" are we referring to the base of our health. In this case indeed, good health depends on circulation, and not just physical, of blood, but also circulation of the emotions, desires, needs, thoughts, astral field, and of our spirit. In this case indeed, health depends on flowing, that our body, our heart, our sex, and our mind allow themselves to change and circulate, do not repress or prohibit anything. Because if we repress something, if we do not allow a part of us (or any of our body) to flow, we generate an obstruction at an astral level, and then indeed problems begin, psychological as well as physical. However, when we speak about working on oneself, developing an awareness, and succeeding to evolve as a being, we should not necessarily let ourselves go or flow with the environment. Perhaps, this work does not go with nature and goes against it. Moreover, while the spark of creation goes from above to below, evolution goes from below to above. Then it could be "normal" that going with the flow is not to evolve.

As this is a book full of lies, I propose that you don't believe me, observe instead. If one does not work on themself and let themselves "flow", perhaps they are following the orders and mandates of their clans (family, friends, school, university, work, culture, religion, society, language, country, continent, world), respecting unfair laws, repeating ill programs, and useless imitations, identifying themself with the opinions of others and their critics, building false personalities based on comparisons, and to "what they will say"; and they live life trapped, from accident to accident, amidst childish superstitions, twisted morals, and useless values; until one day they die (or the body through which they experience this life does). How will this not happen?

Different orders and mandates reach you from each of the clans, often contradictory to each other and none of them belonging to you (the only one that can belong to you arises from your essential being, not the dictation of something external to you) and if you identify yourself and pay attention to everything said to you, then, you stay trapped and far from what you wanted for yourself. Add to the equation a society with the emotional age of a four-year-old child, that just wants to love and be loved, that is able of doing anything and going against its own being to receive love (who begs for love receives alms of love); or that things do not work out as they expected, then they become full of resentment, regret, and guilt, living life, cursing the world. This being, trapped for listening to the outside and not the inside, finishes school and studies what they do not want to, finishes university and does what they do not want to, leaves work and lives with someone they do not want to in a place they do not want to, finishes life and dies as they do not want to. This is how a person who lives a life that does not belong to them, a life that does not correspond to him, ends up thanks to following the current of a suffering world.

If you work on yourselves, you will perhaps discover that you encounter more 'no' than 'yes', that your family, your friends, your colleagues, and your environment do not necessarily sustain your changes, that the social conditions of the world where you live do not favor your individuality, that the education you receive does not encourage you to fulfill yourselves, etc. It is even possible that you "casually" find yourselves with someone you do not know, who will also tell you no! It could be that the world resists you. Because they are all going with the herd and you are becoming the black sheep, who do not go with the flow, who do not do what they are told to do.

Then I meet someone who tells me: "Nobody supports me", still expecting unconsciously that their mother spoil them and their father protect them. Those who do not want to work on themselves, who do not want to get themselves involved in this, usually cling violently to their tragedies; they lift them up as trophies and anecdotes to show the world, to boast about "their limits" based on "their story". Maybe, and just maybe, if they would de-identify themself a little from "their limits" and "their story" they would discover that if they want, they can.

I once met a person who told me: "I am doing it but it's a fight". Who said that it was a fight? As I write this book, I am paying careful attention to expose this as a work and not as a fight. And, in the case that you believe working on something you like is fighting, perhaps, it would be useful to change that definition for playing – or even better, may it function without definition -. At the beginning of this text, I spoke to you of our ways forms of acting in the world (word, thought, and physical act); if you send the order to the universe that the work with yourselves is a fight, I suggest you buy a helmet and prepare for war.

However, if you do this work, you will also see that your vision concerning 'no' and 'yes' changes; that now that you are working on yourselves you are grateful, that there is nobody against you, that 'no' belongs to those who manifest it. Perhaps it is not about fighting, but about accepting. The environment where you move says 'no': do not fight, do not defend, just continue your work on yourselves. Neither fighting, nor rejecting, nor taking it; it is about accepting all opinions without identifying with them, cultivating a sacred indifference as protection to continue your work.

Maybe, and just maybe, evolution is not part of the divine plan that rules you so much. If someone always lets themself go and does nothing, then they flow like a dead fish; they work mechanically like a robot; mandates arrive and they accomplish them; what parents, bosses, friends, society, religion say reaches; they do it during all their life and finally, they die. Perhaps, evolving is about breaking that; performing a very strong work at an internal level, where one observes themself, spins and says I am going to another side, I am going to make my own decisions, look for myself, to become myself. This work I am proposing here is not free (it does not conceive itself), but it must be done to make it possible; educating the mind is the fundamental tool for its success. It is not about avoiding what we do not like and distancing ourselves in some false commodity but instead working with the set that composes us. Maybe, and just maybe, in doing this you will discover a marvelous and possible life, where all decisions possess an immense strength relating to what you want, desire, need, feel, and think.

2. HOWEVER WE TAKE IT, WE LIVE IT

Four friends spoke about the possibility of going for dinner at a new restaurant that had been inaugurated in the neighborhood. The one who had proposed the idea was pointing out to her friends that it was interesting to try something new, for them to see how it was, that it was Martian food and that it was calling her attention. The second answered that she did not want to try something new, that she felt fine with the restaurant where they used to go and that she did not want to go anywhere else. The third was indecisive. The fourth said that she would go where they all wanted to go.

One positive point of view, one negative, one doubtful, and another neutral. The event is the same: going to eat at the new restaurant. Each of them experiences the situation as they perceive it. The first sees the positive side: guided by love, she dares to go beyond the known field to discover something new. The second sees the negative side: guided by fear, she prefers to protect the field where she finds herself and does not want to leave the commodity where she has settled. The third is doubting, she does not listen to what she feels and lets herself be guided by external voices, she is dazed by the possibilities and still does not dare to decide. The fourth is impartial, she can enjoy both restaurants: she dares to try the new and is also fine if they go to the usual. The event is the same and the possibilities are the same, the difference of how each of them live the experience function according to how they take it mentally.

A couple goes on a weekend trip to visit some friends living in the countryside. Whilst they travel, he feels at ease because he sees the journey as a possibility of renewal, to reconnect with nature, to do something different, and to relax. She feels dissatisfied because she sees the journey as distancing from the city, where she has her world, her habits, and customs, where the things she does and the activities she likes are.

He observes toward the future, she toward the past. He pays attention to where they are going and takes it positively. She pays attention to the place they are leaving and takes it negatively. The event is the same, they are both in the same vehicle, they left the same city and are going toward the same countryside. The difference between what one and the other experience happen according to where their attention is placed (he forward and she backward) and how they are charging each of the situations (he observes it positively and she negatively). The event is the same and the possibilities are the same, the difference of how each of them live the experience lies in how they take it mentally.

Two friends are at a party on the terrace of a high building. One tells the other that he is impressed by the height where they find themselves. They both look down silently, they lift their heads and realize the view to the city from the terrace. Whilst they observe, one is contemplating the wonder of human construction, the great spectacle in front of them; he sees humanity's history contained in front of his eyes, he recognizes that it is all a part of progress and enjoys what he sees. The other is thinking about jumping from the terrace.

The first of the friends is contemplating free from the past; he is not reviewing his story nor being held by any memory; he is simply observing the beauty of life dancing in front of his eyes. The second of the friends does not see what he has in front of his eyes, he does not notice it, but he is projecting it as a possibility to escape the problems where he is trapped; he is loaded by his story, he does not see a way out and considers suicide as an option. The event is the same and the possibilities are the same, the difference of how each of them live the experience lies in how they take it mentally.

If the body is the earth, the mind is the planet. If intellect is breathing, the mind is air. If sex is fire, the mind is the sun. If emotions are the waves, the mind is the ocean. The mind is our fundamental tool. We would not be here if it were not for it. The mind is what forms matter. Our will carried out through the thinking, the word, and the deed is the direct result of mental power. If we educate the mind it will be our greatest ally. If we do not educate it, it will be our greatest enemy.

The difference between an educated and non-educated mind is immense. An educated mind uses its thoughts consciously, administrates its vital energy efficiently, educates the heart, concentrates desires, takes care of the body, decides what it wants to do, where it wants to go, chooses a direction, and organizes the resources at its disposal within each present moment to progress. In summary: the mind is marvelous for defining objectives, deciding directions, and organizing. A non-educated mind digs and digs, wastes vital energy, creates problems, is suspicious, limits itself, defines itself by its beliefs and becomes their slave, holds crazy ideas, transforms adversity into misfortune, challenges into tragedies, and inevitably leads toward suffering. An educated mind will make the effort to increase discernment, will learn to doubt in order to expand, and decide in order to progress, it will use its instability as a source of inspiration, it will work to recognize what is hidden in the subconscious, it will de-identify its ego from limiting ideas and this will make it expand to an understanding of the entire universe. A non-educated mind becomes despaired when facing volatility, it does not recognize anything and becomes a victim of its subconsciousness, it has poor discernment, it suffers when in doubt, and can hardly decide, it cultivates limits, and its ego remains rigid and small. An educated mind lives in a state of eternal presence, it is thoughtful and able to enter the world of concentration every time it decides to do so, fulfilling all its objectives, to later return to its state of annihilation in full present. A non-educated mind occupies time on agitation and dispersion, it lives in repetitive thought, in the memory that binds, in limiting identification and restless suffering.

The type of life experienced by each depends a great deal on the degree of development of their intellectual, emotional, sexual, and physical centers. The spirit, to do this work, counts on its main tool: the mind.

The events are the same and the possibilities are the same, the difference of how everyone lives the experience lies in how they take it mentally. We all come equipped with a physical, sexual, emotional, and mental body. We all have a day of approximately twenty-four hours and a week of approximately seven days. The difference of what some or others experience responds to how each of them take what has been lent to them and what they do with it. Everything changes constantly. Nothing remains. All is ours. Nothing belongs to us.

3. UTILITIES OF THE MIND

The mind is wonderful for performing three activities: defining objectives, deciding directions, and organizing.

Defining objectives. What am I going to do now? Write this text. What is my objective with this text? To write simply, clearly, and precisely about the activities for which the mind is especially useful. I defined the objective in my mind and now I release, I let myself somehow be led by the mind and I see how it is guiding me, which are the words coming to it, and how they come to bring me to this objective. Words and elements come to this powerful mind, then I go on to decide directions. What path shall I take to write this paragraph? I choose one and keep walking, I keep writing the paragraph. Suddenly, I stop because a doubt arises: do I feel comfortable writing this phrase or do I look for another possibility? I stop in front of the doubt: what other options do I have? The mind in swift manner presents to me other options to describe the same that I want to describe, with other words in different types of phrases. What is happening here is that I put myself to organize the elements before me, it gives me options to decide on. I select this phrase, taking a new direction, and I retake the writing rhythm. Since we begin our day, the mind keeps defining objectives: brushing your teeth, having a bath, getting dressed, going to work, etc.

The objective is defined and then I let myself go; the mind is going to carry me there. I define a direction then I pass on to another: I allow myself to change. In the meantime, I organize all the tools present that are brought by the mind to lead me through these directions toward the set objective. I work with my mind to develop it. What do I want? Where do I want to go? What do I want to do? How do I want to do it? With whom do I want to be? What do I want to study? Where do I want to study? How do I want to study? Where do I want to live? How do I want to live? etc. The mind is spectacular for this. It is a great ally which, if educated and trained, can lead us where we want.

What is the greatest thing we can create? The most powerful and evolved? Another human being. We cannot do it alone; we need the two polarities: a man and a woman. However, we do not do it all; we intervene in a very small part. The only thing we know how to do is to put the part that corresponds to each (sperm, ovule) and, once the ovule has been fecundated, give the nest good conditions for the child to be born healthy. We do not know how to make it so that the sperm and the ovule come together and perform all the internal processes, we have no clue how to create another human being. If we were given a packet of kidneys, bowels, veins, kilos of skin and bones, a brain, a heart and some other viscera, and were to ask us to create a human being, we could hardly do it. Not even the most advanced technology can achieve it. What we do know is how to give the required conditions for the superior intelligence to do its work. Because that is what happens; here, there is a superior intelligence working through us and, if we do correctly what little we are able to control, it will bring to the world another human being. Now then: if with the help of this mysterious party we can create something as complex and advanced as a child, what can we not create?

Set an objective, whatever it is, possible or not so much, and start working on that, deciding directions and organizing at each instant, at every moment that you are living, all the resources at your disposal to advance toward that objective. The mind is wonderful here, it will be our useful guide. Along the way, allow yourselves to modify directions. The directions can change as you go on: you will know that the most direct way between two points is not necessarily a straight line. And, once you have started to work, you will see that what is important is not so much the achievement in itself, but the process to achieve it. You will see that is not so much about finding, but searching. The journey is what occupies us, opens up possibilities, inspires us, that offers us purposes to develop, to grow, and evolve as human beings.

4. RISKS OF THE MIND

On the other hand, the mind can do things that are useless and affect us negatively on the journey. Its powers are at our disposal; having access to them does not mean that we know how to do things well. Moreover, the opposite tends to happen; some people use mental powers to harm themselves and to go through a life of suffering.

The non-educated mind, or the uncontrolled mind, is going to generate problems, dig, repeat, limit itself, waste available vital energy, suspect, define itself by beliefs, enslave itself, keep insane ideas, lead us unavoidably toward suffering.

Just as it is capable of defining useful objectives, if it is not educated and its parts and operating systems are not worked on, it is capable (at an unconscious level) of defining objectives that go against oneself. The uncontrolled mind will put obstacles in our way. And, if it is not educated, it is going to confer these obstacles to divine fate, without seeing that they by themselves have been placing them.

We count on a vital energy that we administer throughout the day: we receive it, accumulate it, deliver it, every day.[1] Just as there are healthy forms of administering that vital energy, there are also other not so healthy ways

---

[1] For more information about vital energy and negative energy, see chapters 2 and 3 from the book Homemade Wisdom, from Lou Couture and Leandro Taub

to do so. Repetitive mental activity and an uncontrolled mental dialogue will lead us to waste a lot of mental energy that we would have available to other bodily functions. A non-educated mind will tire us.

Moreover, if you observe yourselves, you will discover that this repetitive mental activity and the inner dialogue usually concern the same subjects; they are repeating the same things. It is an activity that wears down and is useless, able to even lead us to obsessions, paranoia, persecutions, suspicions, and other vicissitudes of similar nature.

An uncontrolled mind does not profit from what is here (in the present), because it cannot be silenced, it is not able to live in the present; it passes time continuously dialoguing with itself without seeing what is happening in its surroundings. If, whilst you read this, you think about something else, you will not be able to understand what you are reading and, if you want to remember it, you will have to read it again more attentively. One can be absent whilst being here doing something. And that happens a lot: they are here but they are not, because they are elsewhere.

An example of the uncontrolled mind is obesity. It is not the result of bad nutrition, strange genes, heavy bones, divine fate, or any other similar insanity; its cause is being absent at a mental level. Those who are overweight usually eat whilst they think about something else, reviewing in their mind some anecdote or fantasy, they do not feel the food entering their body (it is more, they do not feel anything) and are unable to recognize if their body has told them 'enough', if it is asking them for another kind of nutrition, if it wants to fast, if it needs liquids, etc. On the other hand, if it were present during the nutrition process, if it were to put its mental attention on the food whilst eating, it would feel again, it would not need to eat until its organism was about to burst, it would instead do it until their body would tell them that is enough, and it would know what food is good for it, what is not, and how to eat.

An uncontrolled mind is going to confer what it does not understand to divine fate; including what it is responsible for and is not allowing itself to recognize. This mind will say: "They were lucky", "She was able to be the actress I always dreamt about but for me that's very far away", "He was able to become a musician and I wasn't", "She was lucky and was able to become a scientist, I wasn't", "He was able to become the writer I wanted to be", "He has money and I do not". The being with an uncontrolled mind will compare, limit themself, will not recognize their strength, direct themself to divine fate, miraculous good and bad luck, to cheap superstitions, to not accepting themself, to judging themself, to not allowing themself, and not giving themself.

Another characteristic of an uncontrolled mind is the snowball effect: a small stone falls from the top of the mountain and, snow rolling down, its size grows whilst descending until it becomes, in the best of cases, a huge ball and, in the worst of cases, a mortal avalanche. The non-educated mind will take an excuse (the small stone on the top of the mountain) and with it will build an enormous tragedy (the size of the huge ball unto the mortal avalanche). This mind is going to dig and dig, suspect, generate problems, and install itself in ongoing suffering.

Another one of the great strengths of an uncontrolled mind is the escape. A mind out of control will always find the form, the excuse, the path, the road, the way to escape. It is not going to recognize what is happening and is going to search for the perfect justification for not being in charge, escaping, and not allowing itself to develop.

Last but not least, a non-educated mind limits. It will identify itself with opinions, points of view, beliefs, definitions, names, habits, customs, mandates, orders, laws, and other rarities; it will solidify in its structure, it will be enslaved by them and will not allow itself to get out. This way, it will build a mountain of limits that will build a life full of impossibilities, inflexibilities, incapacities, suffering, and "bad luck".

5. PARTS OF THE MIND

The mind can be split into four parts: the unstable mind, the intellect, the subconscious, and the ego. The unstable mind doubts, the intellect decides, the subconscious holds, and the ego identifies itself. We need the unstable mind to expand and the intellect to advance, whilst from the good game between the subconscious and the ego, we develop our consciousness (and from the uncontrolled use of both, our unconsciousness). What an educated mind does with the dialogue between the unstable mind and the intellect is doubting and solving, over and over again. What an uncontrolled mind does is avoid the dialogue between the parts; it doubts and never solves or does not allow itself to doubt and never expands; it does not dare make decisions or decide without daring to doubt. What an educated mind does with the dialogue between the subconscious and the ego is recognize what is held, de-identify from it and go beyond. What an uncontrolled mind does is avoid the dialogue between the parts: it does not recognize anything and identifies itself with rigid definitions hosted in the deep of the subconscious.

6. THE UNSTABLE MIND

Those who doubt everything do little, those who doubt nothing learn little.

The unstable mind is the part of the mind that allows us to doubt. It is the part of the mind that installs us in volatility; it offers alternatives, is able to access the field of infinite options, and it positions instability (is necessary to advance if used properly). It is the part of the mind that can go beyond our control, the reality behind our reality, where everything that was, is, and will be is summed in one moment. If I were speaking of the tarot, I would say that it is a mix between the Nameless Arcana, The Fool, and the Arcana I, The Magician. It is what offers us chaos, infinite possibilities, and madness. It is what offers us the great options menu to choose from, where everything is always possible previous to action. It is what opens up possibilities. If I were speaking about numbers, I would say that it is a mix between the number zero and one. It is nothingness, the lack of order, where there is no where and when there is no when; the eternal beginning, that offers to start again over and over; the first appearance, the first thought, the genesis, the unity that contains all. It is the part of the mind that doubts; allowing us to see beyond the known and the established in our present to, afterwards, allow us to define objectives and decide directions. Without doubt we would not be able to move on, and neither can we by doubting all the time.

For this reason, one of the forms of which wisdom is defined in Hebrew is the ability of auto-annulment. The wise is the one who is constantly annulling; not another, or themself; but their established knowledge. They learn something; they understand it, feel it, comprehend it; and then they annul it to allow the entrance of something new. Over and over again. Doubt, when properly worked on, is what allows us to go beyond any known universe. Those who do not doubt, do not annul, do not allow space in their mind for the new to come in. On the other side, those who doubt everything and do not solve those doubts, neither annul nor allow themselves to advance. Doubt removes us from pre-established knowledge and allows us to see beyond. It does this precious work with us. Once the options are open, to advance beyond the known universe, we resort to another part of the mind: the intellect. The intellect decides, it is the one that can guide our will. It is then that our doubt opens up and we solve it to advance through the deciding intellect: the doubt arises, our observational field opens up, the intellect intervenes by deciding, we succeed in moving on.

If there are doubts left unsolved, if we open up the field but neither decide to advance nor return, we remain installed in the instability that functions as a drain of vital energy: taking away vitality and installing a negative emotion in us and the environment. Staying within the unstable mind is staying in complete madness, in all possibilities, the chaos that erodes order, the reason without reason; the possibilities that open up remain as if they are nonexistent because none are triggered through decision. If we lodge within the unstable mind, we will see the parts of madness, where control and order are lost. It is useful to have doubts, always and when they are resolved. Some tools for resolving doubts are to not neglect them, express them correctly, include others, listen to what is felt (and not so much what is analyzed), ask for answers, and to avoid regret.

On the opposite side, not allowing ourselves to access the unstable mind causes us not to open up, not to doubt, not to leave our own image and rigid point of view, to stay immobile in a defined and closed state, to abandon ourselves in a comfort zone that will inevitably transform into false comfort if we do not advance. At some point, that instability could have been gratifying, however with time moving on, the being also does – and if it does not allow it, problems begin -. If the being does not advance, stability stagnates: if water does not flow, it bogs; if food is not eaten, it rots; if a house is not inhabited, it falls into pieces; if money is not invested, it is devaluated. Doubt is very useful and very risky. If we do not use it, we can remain solidified with a rigid image of ourselves, in a world where we do not allow ourselves to change. Never accessing the unstable mind makes us abandon ourselves in a too rational, too squared world where nothing new can appear, where things are as they are and cannot go beyond. We need instability to dare to go a step beyond.

Progress is pendular: doubting, deciding, progressing, establishing; over and over again. We advance between the unstable and the stable, we need to decide as well as to accumulate, to burst as well as to stabilize, to see beyond and establishing ourselves, to propose objectives and to achieve them, to go through crisis and solve them. It is about going step by step, neither from left to left nor from right to right; step by step, with both legs. In our life, everything in its just measurement is precious (and in exaggeration is an addiction); going from one side to another as a pendulum allows us to trigger and stabilize, progressing through the dialogue between polarities. Instability, when properly worked on, will help us advance (odd numbers, masculine polarity). Stability, when properly worked on, will help us stabilize (even numbers, feminine polarity). When we exaggerate to one of both sides, an unmeasured tension is generated and problems arise. As life itself. Thus, addictions arise.[2]

One day, while writing, I began to look through the window. While the letters were progressing, the clouds also did. When I stopped writing, I saw that the clouds were not moving anymore. It drew my attention, but I did not realize the connection until I repeated the experiment. I wrote again and the clouds were moving. I stopped writing and the clouds stopped. What an imminent force I had met! I was afraid that if I got up from the chair, if I stopped doing it, it would stop happening. I was afraid that if I got out of the dream, the clouds would stop following my writing. So, I continued writing. For hours and hours. While I was writing, I put my attention on the waves of clouds that even followed the rhythm of my writing. When I hit the keys, the clouds formed peaks; when I treated the keys gently, the clouds formed smooth waves; when I wrote quickly, the clouds moved fast and when I did it slowly, the clouds did the same; when I stopped writing, the clouds stopped their movement again. The experience was wonderful. So I went on and went on writing, by then, more attentive to the clouds than to the writing itself, creating a

---

[2] For more information about vices, see chapter 2 of Leandro Taub's book Holy Devil.

dialogue between my fingers and the clouds; drawing shapes and figures in the sky through the letters. The phrases went from prose to poetry, the text esthetics changed; now I was doing everything to please those beautiful clouds, dedicated to beautifying them more and more. Hours went by and I was still sitting in the chair, in front of the computer, making collages of clouds in the sky, forming phrases, songs, and paintings. Suddenly, I heard someone knock on the door. The cloud movement stopped, my attention changed its focus, my gaze turned to the door, my heart was beating fast, I breathed deeply and turned my gaze to the computer whilst someone was knocking on the door again. On the screen, just one phrase could be seen, repeated thousands and thousands of times: "I am going toward you".

What you just read arouse spontaneously because I accessed the unstable mind through the intellect which, efficiently, decided to do so. Without asking myself how, or why, what I did was leave my comfort zone, accessing the unstable mind (which does not know limits and definitions) and, through the ego that defines and the intellect deciding that I have to flow, together with some memories housed in my subconscious, I let myself go and see what I could literally "invent". I wrote while improvising. It was an unplanned moment. I went to the unstable mind to look for what I could write from there, without even thinking about it. And what you just read was what happened.

If you house yourself in the unstable mind all the time, you are installed in madness, in non-order, using a laptop as a hat and a freshly baked cake as a pillow could be very normal. However, if you access it when you need to and then come back, you will discover that the unstable mind is also the one translating our creativity –born in our sexuality -. While our sexuality is the one that creates – from a child up to a new hairstyle, any form of creativity arises from our sex -, the unstable mind is our mental filter through which we access such creativity. It is a dubbing of our creativity. Going there will offer us alternatives. Although not knowing how or being afraid, when daring, one discovers that there is more beyond what is there. If one is accessing the unstable mind, different forms of seeing the same things will be found; one will be installed in infinite points of view, mental openness, options, possibilities, thinking out of the box. It is the part of the mind able to get out of the box – the known world – and travel the uncertain. If you decide to explore it, you will discover wonderful worlds: Alice in Wonderland, Yellow Submarine, Dream Number 9, Star Trek, science fiction adventures, all that can be and beyond. You leave the box, you transform the box, you build the box, you make the box disappear, you see the box in a fourth and fifth dimension. Within the unstable mind everything becomes an option.

As a tool of practice, I propose you try it, see by yourselves how it works; write five lines on a sheet letting yourselves go, without a pre-established course, and if the idea comes, change it, allow yourselves to see where intuition performing through the unstable mind leads you.

Those who want to write or create something artistic are generally full of plans and rarely carry them out. Sometimes, it is not about more than, once the aim has been set, allow oneself to be and flow with the mental game; deciding the direction and seeing how the mind organizes the elements that are presented to guide us toward that objective. Great artworks began like this; they were built as they were done.

7. THE INTELLECT

The intellect is the part of the mind that decides. It has the capacity of developing an intelligence, discovering the utility of things – a mind that trains itself with the help of the unstable mind can even change the function of things -, discerning, organizing, separating, interpreting, and reasoning. It is the part of the mind that animals do not possess. The intellect is our scientific and analytical mind. It is the one that handles our will. It is the one that knows how to choose. It is the one that decides.

Every decision, whether it be conscious or unconscious, had to be done from the intellect to be made possible. Do whatever you may, be it conscious or unconscious, it can be done thanks to the existence of an intellect that gives the order, that makes the decision to do so.

While the unstable mind allows us to open up our field of action and access other possibilities, the one that selects, that decides, that pushes us to act is the intellect. It is the part of the mind that gives the order for us to do.

The intellect can have distinct levels of development. The undeveloped intellect results in a weak will. This kind of willpower will be easily guided by a superior will telling it what to do and what not to. It will cost for a weak will to do by itself and then, as a result, it will obey what it is told to do. It will do what another superior volition tells it to do. Think of the child in front of his father and mother, the youth at school, the adolescent with his friends, the adult facing society and laws, the believer before religion.

The unconscious superior willpower will tell the inferior will what to do. Except when it transgresses. The more we develop our intellect, the more it increases, the greater the power of the will and the capacity to make decisions without depending on another. An educated mind will work to increase its capacity of discernment and intelligence, strengthening its willpower up to the point where, maybe one day, it will only respond to itself.

The intellect is the one that decides, working through an intimate relationship with the unstable mind. When the unstable mind offers the doubt, the intellect has the opportunity to decide before the presented options. A developed intellect will dare to make decisions, one time and again, although they may imply the transgression of past stability. A little developed intellect will not dare to make decisions to progress and will cling to previous established knowledge.

8. THE SUBCONSCIOUS

The subconscious is our trunk; the one keeping instinct and memory. It is the part of the mind that performs as a backpack, where we gather the things that we do not let ourselves forget, the things we recognize just as well as the things we do not recognize. We house everything that we do not allow to pass and have retained in some form in the subconscious.

Our psychological backpack, the subconscious, is where we accumulate everything we are told and what we identify ourselves with; what happened to us as we were children and determined who we are; the failed relationship we identify ourselves with; the frustration with our expectations with which we identify ourselves; the solidified attachment we identify ourselves with; the social, cultural, religious mandate we identify ourselves with. It is the hard disk of our computer. It is what saves things.

A therapist usually guides the patient to help them recognize what they have housed in the subconscious. Their work is to help one recognize themself. Because, when we do not recognize what we have kept there, it subjects us and affects us without us knowing it. The way we talk, the way we move, the way we breathe, the way we eat, the way we think, the way we sleep, the way we relate, the way we do what we do; everything is being influenced by what we have kept in the subconscious. If we recognize it, we can remove it or maintain it. If we do not recognize it, it remains present.

Therefore, the work done by a mind training its subconscious is recognizing what it saves. Recognizing until, at some moment, we recognize ourselves. To no further advance the rigid thoughts housed in the subconscious, it is necessary to work in order to recognize what is saved there. And it is not just about that, this does not end with recognition. After recognizing; work for the other parts of the mind begin to appear, the ego: de-identifying oneself from those memories with which the mind, consciously or unconsciously, had identified itself with.

If there is some illness, problem, affectation, repetition, or any other kind of reaction, it is because there is something housed in the subconscious that is making noise. The initial work will be to turn around and explore the shadow, recognizing what is behind of what there is: why what is affecting us is affecting us. Through this self-observation one is able to recognize themselves, discovering their psychological nerves. Once the memory housed in the subconscious, boosting the affectation, is recognized, the next phase can be accessed: de-identification. When doing this work, the being stops behaving as a victim of that nerve (the memory saved in the subconscious) and can go on to tame the memory and even heal it. If there is no recognition, the affectation occurs without knowing where it comes. If there is recognition, there is possibility of control. When the memory dominates and is not recognized, there is a submission of the being without them knowing how, why, or where it is. They feel that something is somehow controlling them, but they are not able to recognize what, how, and where. They feel that something controls them, but they do not understand it; they do not know it, because they do not see it.

If the mind is uncontrolled and little educated, not only will it not recognize the memories saved in the subconscious, but it will practically be unaware of what happens; it will think that it is the victim of divine fate, escaping from any possibility of responsibility for oneself. It will be unaware that something is housed in the subconscious and, sometimes, it will not even feel the affectation. Some are so deeply programmed that they have stopped paying attention to themselves and are far from discovering how they feel. When a few daring individuals allow themselves to approach the present, even a little, they will be able to feel. If they are able to feel, at least they will rediscover that they have affectations and alterations at all levels; then, they will be able to ask themselves: Why did this happen to me? What is happening to me? How do I feel? Of course, they will not yet have the answers, but at least they will have taken a great step; they will have jumped from the unconsciousness and deep programming to feeling. And now that they feel, if they work on educating their mind, they will be able to turn around and explore their shadow; recognizing what they have saved in the subconscious, becoming aware of things they did not allow themselves to see and getting to know themselves.

It would be like walking with shoes without seeing them. Some think that their true feet are those they are using now (including the shoe), that their real height is the one they have now (increased by the shoe sole), that their true inclination is the one they have now (including the inclination forward provoked by the heel of the shoe). They are absolutely identified with the shoe, believing that it is part of their essential being without recognizing that it is something they sometime put on and that, as they put it on, they can also take off. However, some feel that their walk is not totally natural, that they are housed in a false commodity and that they do not walk as freely as they would like to. Then, they begin to investigate themselves, observing themselves, until one day they understand that they are wearing shoes. Returning to the present made them feel and discover that they were not comfortable with their walk, which boosted them to observe and search themselves. Recognizing that you are wearing shoes does not take them off, but at least allows you to discover from where the affectation they feel is coming from. Then another type of being arrives, the one that trained their mind even more, and they not only allow themself to feel and observe themself to recognize themself, but they also dare to go on their knees, undo their laces and take off their shoes. A miracle! Now they discover a more beautiful and practical walk, they feel the earth under their feet again; they discover that the leather feet they had before were false and find their true feet; they discover that the previous height was false and find their real height; they discover that their previous inclination was false and find their true inclination. Then someone who has progressed even more on training their mind appears (who uses it as a tool to develop their awareness): not only do they take off their shoes, they also discover that those feet are not "their" feet; that that body is not "their" body; that there is still something beyond this and that they are able to explore it. They de-identify themself from the recognized, forget themself, and surrenders to being without not-being.

There are those who ask for help, however when they receive it they resist recognizing. I have met dozens of people that consult me on something and when I answer they run away terrified, they get angry at me, they defend themselves thinking that I am attacking them, or they even answer by attacking me verbally or physically. Those who do not want to recognize will see the solicited help as aggression. However, the task is not in the other (one cannot heal the other), the task of a trained mind is in oneself, in looking at the mirror (not just physic, but also oneiric) and observing oneself. Recognizing everything done, said, and thought; because the subconscious comes to light through all the clothes of the soul (thought, word, and physical act).

There is something peculiar in the exercise I proposed in the section about the unstable mind, concerning writing five lines improvised. If you do it frequently, you will discover that there are words and forms that are repeated; it is exactly there where something housed in the subconscious comes to light (in this case, through the act of writing). What is saved in the subconscious is asking to be recognized, it emerges constantly and shows itself through all the possible ways it can find. Repetitions, affectations, and reactions are the subconscious ways of speaking. Where a pattern is accomplished, there is something. Where there is a reaction, there is something. Where there is an emotional affectation, there is something. If one escapes, it will reappear. If one fights, it is nourished and it is strengthened. Daring to play with psychological viscera, investigating deeply, traveling through darkness, is useful to discover what is housed in the subconscious – to recognize it, to de-identify ourselves from it and regain freedom -. Releasing what does not belong to us to discover what does – if you were able to take something that is not yours, you will also be able to release it -. It is about abandoning the false self to discover the essential self.

9. THE EGO

The ego is the identification with the image we have of ourselves. The ego is the one identifying, comparing and defining itself from the definitions that it gives to itself.

It is neither good nor bad. The mind, our great tool, can be split into four parts, and the ego is one of them. Therefore, it is absurd that some people try to eliminate the ego; get rid of it, kill it, eradicate it from their lives. It would be like cutting off an arm. This will not make the arm disappear (because at an astral level, the arm will still exist, and the person will be able to feel it). We are in a time of the world where we can hear "no ego". How "no ego"? Does anyone say, "no stomach" or "no blood"? We are in a time where we can also hear "no mind". How "no mind"? Does anyone say, "no heart", "no sex" or "no body"? Yes, some deny the ego, deny the mind, deny the heart, some even deny the sex. But let us try another alternative: there is no bad ego, but an untrained ego; the ego is wonderful: where we lead it, depends on our mental education and training. Let's try this: Say yes to the educated mind; yes, to the de-identified ego; yes, to the concentrated sex; yes, to the giving and receiving heart.

The ego is our mental mirror. It is the identification with the image we have from ourselves; it is the identification we have put on ourselves and with which we have made an agreement, considering ourselves to being that. Perhaps you have heard the following phrases: "I am not anxious", "I am Spanish", "I am dark-skinned", "I am tall", "I am unstable", "I am obese", "I am from such a football team", "I am a vegetarian", "My favorite color is violet", "My favorite food is bread", "I am a writer", "I cannot", "I am good, she is bad", and a long list of etcetera, etcetera. The ego is what defines us and identifies itself with that definition. It is what projects a mental image about oneself and is defined by it. It is the identification with our own mental mirror. It is even the ego acting through myself at the very moment I write these lines, defining how things are (to some extent, it is also therefore that at the beginning of this book I warned that everything I was going to say would be a lie).

An uncontrolled mind will have a small and limited ego; this is a very rigid and solidified identification with a limited image of ourselves. This kind of ego will identify itself with points of view, opinions, tastes, beliefs, habits, morals, mandates, manners and forms, with definitions of the world and its false self. This kind of ego is trapped in a castle of definitions, between what it likes and what not.

An educated and trained mind will be expanding its ego beyond its rigid identifications, de-identifying itself from that limited image it has from itself and expanding its observation field by identifying itself with what is beyond oneself (thus, discovering that it forms a part of oneself). If you look at yourself, you will discover that you are perhaps not anxious, but that it is an operating mode due to lack of education; that perhaps you are not Spanish, American, English, Asian, etc. but that the body through which you experience life with was born in an area of this planet that has a name since a few hundred years ago, and that maybe it will not have it anymore in a few hundred years more; that perhaps you are not from the world, but you are the world (and why not, the universe as well); that perhaps you don't have a preferred food, but that there is one food that you like because you eat it in fair measure, feeling and associating it with a pleasurable memory (but if you abuse it or eat it absent-mindedly, maybe you will not like it anymore); that maybe you are not writers, lawyers, sportsmen, scientists, etc. but rather that it is about the activities that you perform; that perhaps you cannot do it if you don't try, and when you try it, you will know; that maybe human beings aren't good or bad, but that every manifested being has a potential to create, maintain and destroy.

The limited ego defines and identifies itself with that definition; the ego is educated and de-identifies itself from the ancient definition and is being expanded by identifying itself with what is beyond, until achieving at a certain point, to comprehend the entire universe, and after that, de-identifying itself completely from the self, in order to be oneself and live in the present.

The uncontrolled mind, with a non-educated ego, limits us. This ego, by identifying itself with its mental image (points of view, opinions, tastes, beliefs, habits, morals, mandates, manners, forms, and others) generates solidifications in the mind and observes the world through these. So, it will not be able to see the world in its greatness, but it will see it as small, within the size of its limits. This mind will become a slave of these solidifications, provoking a small and limited world, the cage in which it will live. This ego will want everything; it will look for recognition, fame and prestige; it will separate itself from the world; it will want everybody to fail, except for itself; it will identify itself with everything it finds (believing that the world revolves around itself); it will just do what is convenient for itself; and it will construct false personalities – with which it will identify itself rigidly – based on comparisons.

Hence, another part of the mind that I mentioned before comes into play: the subconscious. A trained mind will recognize what it has lodged in the subconscious and will de-identify the ego from those memories and instincts. The educated mind will de-identify the ego from any definition, and will identify itself with the uncertain, achieving to enlarge the world where it lives and expand itself.

The uncontrolled mind, with a limited ego, is small and rigid, and it will not just project mental images with which it will feel identified, but will repeat it throughout the day, exposing its definition to the world. This ego will want to expose itself. This uncontrolled mind will say to the world: "I am shy, don't make me talk to more than one person, because if I do, I will explode from timidness", or "I am bipolar, this is why I need to take daily thirty-three sleeping tablets", "I am free, this is why I smoke fifteen kilograms of marijuana per day". The "I am" and their alternatives adapt themselves very well to the vocabulary of a small ego, clinging continuously, defining itself and defining the world. And it is not even aware of the mandates it is sending to the universe! If whilst progressing through your day, you remember the "clothes" of the soul (thoughts, words and actions), you will discover that everything you say, think and do is an order you are launching: that there is a casual web set by yourselves in your constant comings and goings, that respond to yourselves; that words have power; that if you repeat "I cannot" you warrant that you will not be able, if you repeat "I am ugly", the world will see you as such, if you repeat "it is difficult", you will not dare.

The other activity that the limited and little trained ego will perform is to go outside. It will not just define 'itself', but it will also define another. It will have a rigid vision of the world that will not be able to bare something beyond its definition. It will not tolerate the uncertainty and the unknown. This ego meets me and says to me: "You are a writer, you are Argentinian, you are Jewish, you are too young, you are indecent and you are mad". If it would train itself, time after it would say: "Writing is what he does; Argentina is the name of the country where he was born; Judaism is the religion with which he was educated; his age is not just physical, but also mental, emotional, sexual and spiritual". This limited ego will hardly see the other by how he is but will see him through the filter of its definitions. It will define its partner, friends, family members, colleagues, relationships, work, artwork (in case of doing one), study, books, society, and the world.

The trained mind, with an ego in a constant de-identification and expansion process, will observe what it thinks, what it says and what it does, to discover that there is something to which it clings or is in process of defining. The trained mind, with an intellect that decides, will guide itself to recognize what it has lodged in the subconscious in order to de-identify its ego from it.

"I am Leandro Taub". Perhaps, I am not Leandro Taub, and this is just the name I use for others to call me on this planet; perhaps, I am not from this planet, but I am in this planet; perhaps, I am not just in this planet, but I am being simultaneously existing as part of the whole universe; perhaps, this is not my body, but the body I am using. The small and limited ego will define itself by its name, document number, country, mandates, cultures, habits, religions, morals, groups of interests, among others.

10. SUMMARY OF THE PARTS OF THE MIND AND ACTIVITIES TO BE DONE BY EACH

- **Unstable mind.** The doubter.

To allow instability in order to open the game. Do not lodge ourselves in the unstable mind or avoid it. Allow ourselves to doubt. Accessing this part every time we need it and the situation requires it. Do not fear it. Allow ourselves to enter instability so that doubt arises which introduces options. Then, with the help of the intellect, resolve the doubt deciding to act by one of its options.

- **Intellect.** The decider.

To decide in order to advance. Work on increasing discernment and mathematical intelligence. Strengthen the will with trust and courage. Develop reason and understanding. Then, lead what is understood towards the feeling to be able to comprehend it; passing intellectual knowledge through the filter of the heart (feelings). Learn to decide, choose, select, without looking back and without regret. Allow the existence of death of the options that were not triggered. Dare to decide. Know that once the selection has been made it was the only one possible.

- **Subconscious**. The keeper.

To recognize in order to know. Practice self-observation day and night, searching for reactions, repetitions, and emotional affections. Observe what is thought, said, and done. Review contradictions. Search until discovering what has been saved. Recognize all the conscious and unconscious memories and instincts.

- **Ego**. The identifier.

De-identifying in order to expand. Once the task of self-observation and recognition of the memories and instincts within the subconscious have been done, de-identify yourselves from them. Come off of definitions and naming what we do not know. Come out of rigor and allowing the expansion of identifying oneself with the uncertain. Dare to experience the uncertainty and the unknown without defining them.

11. WAYS OF ACTING

The mind has five ways of acting: agitation, dispersion, attention, concentration, and annihilation. While the four parts of the mind described in the previous section perform as isolated and related pieces, working between them and influencing each other, each keeping their independent tasks, the five modes of operating perform progressively, like steps, progressing from one to another, successively. The first two are the most primitive (that generate the most problems), while the following three lead us progressively to situations of well-being (the last achieves a state of continuous ecstasy).

An uncontrolled mind will jump in between the ways of acting according to the internal and external stimuli it receives: reactions, affections, repetitions (at an internal level), and words, thoughts, acts, and stronger wills that guide it (at an external level). An educated and trained mind will be able to focus its attention on the most convenient way of acting at every moment. The uncontrolled mind tends to be between the two ways of acting that carry the most instability and problems (agitation and mental dispersion), while the educated and trained mind will work in order to be between both ways of acting that bring the most stability and well-being (concentration and mental annihilation). The uncontrolled mind will perform by the emergency of the situation, useless programming, or the lack of will that guides it: the examination arrives, it becomes concentrated; nobody watches it, it goes into agitation, it is hungry, it acts; nothing to do, it entertains itself, and disperses; and so, over and over again. The educated and trained mind will act according to the requirements of the situation, it will be in a constant present (mental annihilation) and if an objective is set, it will advance towards it attentively and with concentration.

12. MENTAL AGITATION

Mental agitation is a mental activity without any specific objective. It is the favorite form of operating for an uncontrolled mind. It is the activity that goes nowhere but does not keep quiet, it is the internal voice that confuses, that bounces about everywhere uncontrollably like a pinball. The two main causes of mental agitation are desires and fear. Based on this way of acting, more than one spiritual discipline has accused the mind of being an enemy. But the mind is not mental agitation, this is simply one of the five acting ways of the mind, the most uncontrolled and primitive; however, there are another four that follow.

You are walking on the street and suddenly become distracted because you have seen a butterfly passing by; you see it fly for a few moments and begin thinking about what it would be like to fly, when suddenly you are surprised by the sound of a car horn because you have been standing in the middle of the road. You keep walking and ask yourself why you did not react towards the aggression of that vehicle, when your phone rings; you answer and it is a friend, you talk for a few minutes. After a few minutes you stop paying attention to him because a pretty girl has passed by; you hang up on your friend and follow the girl for a few meters, imagining what you will do to introduce yourself to her, when suddenly you are captivated by a smell. You turn around and, following the smell, you think about how good some food would be. You discover a bakery, go inside, buy some bread, and leave thinking about having a drink. After walking a few blocks, remember-

ing the tasks you have to do for work, your phone rings. It is your friend telling you that you left her behind at the local when you told her that you were leaving for a moment to buy a drink. You turn to see where you are, because you do not have a clue where you have been walking, and due to your hurry you stumble over a raised tile.

This would be a mind acting by mental agitation while walking on the street. It has no order and no self-control. If it has objectives, they are forgotten, but it is not silent; it is pure mental uncontrolled activity, constant distraction. It is the mind acting without an objective, in agitation (ephemeral objectives can appear for seconds, before being replaced by the next). In this form of acting, the mind will perform according to arising stimuli, internal just as much as external. In the case of the story I told, the stimuli were the butterfly; what flying would be like, the horn; the resentment, the phone; the pretty girl, the smell of bread; the fictitious hunger; the fictitious thirst; the anxiety, and the things to be done. The mind will be hyperactive, responding to the stimuli that arises.

This way of acting brings us instability, installs unstable emotions into the environment (usually resulting in negative emotions), it is chaotic, it is not controlled, it is not tamed, it is not channeled, it does not organize, and it leads anywhere.

It is the least efficient way of acting of the mind and, paradoxically, is the most frequently used by an uncontrolled mind. As it does not define objectives, or choose directions, or organize, or know how to silence itself, or keep itself present, this mind will be going anywhere, from stimulation to stimulation, firing thoughts toward all directions: remembering things, imagining, projecting, expecting, observing, expounding, judging, excessively talking, confusing the world and confusing itself. There is no possible activity to be done from this way of acting. If it is begun, it is abandoned after a few moments; if something is being done, it is done without attention; if it is being completed, it will never actually be done. In this way of acting, the mind keeps traveling in time (imaginations and projections between the past and the future) and dedicates a minimal and meager moment to the present time. It is the way of acting of a mind where all accidents and failures occur.

13. MENTAL DISPERSION

Mental dispersion is the way of acting of the mind that follows mental agitation. The mind will remain uncontrolled, but now a point has emerged, an average, a center, an objective to be reached. However, in this way of operating, the goal remains unattainable.

To those who have at some point studied statistics this word will be familiar: dispersion. For mathematicians, dispersion can be easily explained through the Gaussian Curve; dispersion indicates the distance between the center of the bell (the average) and the sides of the bell, to each degree or level of confidence. To simply explain it, dispersion would be the distance between the sides of the bell and its center: to what degree the center is dispersed from itself. It is used as a tool to calculate probabilities. Now then, mental dispersion is similar to mathematical dispersion: it measures the distance from the center. The center would be the goal set consciously or unconsciously to the mind; the distance, all activity still surrounding it (close as well as far) from this center.

Mental dispersion is still far from concentrating, it has not even gathered the mental waves; uncontrolled, repetitive, and chaotic mental activity continues to exist. Nevertheless, it is more advanced than mental agitation because it has already incorporated a point: the objective has been defined.

You arrive at Civic Education class. The professor begins to explain a load of laws and, as you have no interest in what is being told to you, you put yourself to observe a class mate that you like; when they see you, you divert your gaze and begin to chat with the friend seated next to you; then you draw on your notebook, check messages on your cellphone, you go to the bathroom seventeen times, look at the time about fifty times, you ask yourself how much is left before the class ends; until the bell rings. You leave and know nothing about what was said in class.

This is what happens in mental dispersion. As there is no interest or as one does not have an educated mind, as defined as the objective may be (in the classroom, theoretically, it would be learning), the mind will go from extreme to extreme, with much mental activity. In this form of operating of the mind, the objective is defined, twenty laps are made around it, castles are built in the sand, there is inner dialogue for hours and then, maybe, there is a return to the objective. Much instability and problems are still generated here. Not even the attention has appeared.

If you want to do a job, build a relationship, carry out some deed, study something, read a book, make a painting, compose a musical theme, or any other objective you propose for yourselves, it will be almost impossible to achieve with the form of mental dispersion. And if something is done, it will be much too poor of a project. Imagine for a moment a relationship in the form of operating of the mind in mental dispersion: you speak to your partner and with luck they hear the first and last word you said, they couldn't pay attention to what happened in between those two words. Imagine for a moment a project on a computer with mental dispersion: you set a goal, you check the social networks 3,657 times, you speak on the phone with more friends than you have, and you return to the project without having done even one tenth of the work you wanted to do. Now imagine reading a book with mental dispersion: you begin to read it and you go to eat something, you come back and scratch one of your feet, you come back and switch on the television, you come back and speak to someone on the phone; as a result, you progress half a chapter in two years. All activity we want to perform with this way of operating will go through a weakened path.

Just as with mental agitation, this way of operating will bring about many problems: lack of control, instability, and mental repetition. The mind without education and control will live in these two forms of operating (agitation and dispersion): if it has nothing to do, it will be on vacation in mental agitation; if it has something to do, it will go to mental dispersion, approaching little by little and poorly to its goal.

14. GATHERING MENTAL WAVES

Here is where the game changes, this is where the forms of operating of the mind that bring stability begin. Mental power increases as it progresses in its ways of operating.

Gathering mental waves is the form of operating of the mind that occurs when we have defined an objective and the intellect has decided to guide the will towards it. Now the mind begins to gather all its waves in the direction of the objective; as the attention is focused, things occur. Now it will be possible to complete a task, build a relationship, work with oneself, and do anything the mind proposes. The mind applies its attention towards a point and, no matter how many distractions there may be, it ceases to be in uncontrolled forms performing in all directions (agitation or mental dispersion).

By gathering mental waves, the Gaussian Curve (that I commented on in the section, "Mental Dispersion") notably shrinks; now the mental activity will surround the objective, it will make us operate in its direction and the margin of error will notoriously decrease (in mental dispersion, the margin of error was huge; the objective could be in the south and one could end up in the north). As mental waves are gathered, the student pays attention in class; they become distracted for a few moments and come back; perhaps, they do not understand everything the teacher says, but his senses point at there. As mental waves are gathered, we can listen to what our partner tells us; we may not notice everything that they insinuate, perhaps we cannot yet listen to what they manifest when they are telling us what they tell us, however, we are able to build a relationship. As mental waves are gathered, we are able to perform the work or tasks that we propose ourselves; it may include various errors and corrections may be done, it may not be what we planned, however, we are able to do it. As mental waves are gathered, we can observe and learn from ourselves; we may not know ourselves completely, we may perhaps not be able to take off all of the fake disguises, however, the attention on ourselves can already do some work. In this way of operating, the mind has the power to achieve.

Imagine a shower throwing water on a bath. In the form of operation of mental agitation, the water would get out of the shower, as well as on the walls, the floor, the mirror, the toilet; in the same way, mental waves circulate all over, uncontrolled. In the way of acting of mental dispersion, there is already an objective; however, it is incapable of being fulfilled. Now the water would indeed pass through the shower, but it would have holes all over (even the tubing), and it would get into the bathtub, just as well as on the sides, and the ceiling. In the way of operating of gathering mental waves, although they can be distracted, the mind points towards one place; the shower would function "normally" and it would succeed in throwing water toward the bathtub, covering all its sectors and possibly wetting the wall and the shower curtain a little. In the next form of operating, concentration, something magical will happen: the shower would become technological, we would be able to move a knob that would concentrate the water flow and instead of going towards the whole bathtub, the water would point to just one direction.

15. CONCENTRATION

Where concentration is applied, the miracle arises.

This is the miracle making mode of the mind. When the mind succeeds in arriving to the form of operating of concentration, spectacular phenomena begin to emerge, time is doubled and the mind is able to do everything that is found beyond what is possible (it makes what seems impossible, possible).

If we retake the image of the Gaussian Curve, we see now that the bell has become so narrow that it seems to only have the inner pendulum; the mind does not wander anymore and is not being entertained by distractions, it applies all its attention in one direction with views of its goal. If we go back to the example of the shower throwing water on the bathtub; now we would be able to move the knob that enables the concentration of the water to flow in just one direction. Have you noticed what happens when you execute this? The amount of water and pressure coming from the tank or pipes is the same as before, it has not changed, however, the stream coming from the shower has much higher pressure than what it had when it was throwing water in all directions. If we put our body in its way, we feel how the impulse of the concentrated water hits our body. The same happens with mental waves. If you concentrate mental waves, huge pressure is generated; and this does not happen because there are now more mental waves than before, but because those existing are concentrated into one direction toward the same objective. Our world changes with this form of operating of the mind. It is going to generate interesting things. This is how a mind performing in concentration mode functions; it succeeds in focusing its mental waves into one direction and its power has a much superior pressure to those experimented on in the previous three ways of operating that we reviewed.

Remember when there was a subject at school that did not interest you and instead of leaving to give useful meaning to the time you had, you stayed in the classroom. The whole academic term went by without you succeeding in paying attention; the mind was between agitation and dispersion, occasionally being able to join mental waves; however, you achieved to know little about the subjects studied during the course. Until one day while talking with a schoolmate you realized that there would be an exam the following week. The urgency of life and death appeared – paradoxically, the causes generating the most stress to human beings in the 21st century are, in first place, the death of a beloved, and second, an exam -, then, the uncontrolled mind was triggered responding to this stimulation. How did it respond? It obligated itself to enter a state of concentration: in one week, thanks to the emergency, the mind was able to concentrate and study for the whole exam within those previous days; you did it and you passed.

Maybe more than one person reading this text has experienced a similar situation to the one just told whether it be in study or in another activity. Did we not ask ourselves what happened? You succeeded in studying and learning a subject that you did not understand during a whole year in just one week (this is being generous, because you usually do it within a few days) and from which you had no clue what it was about. What happened was that, due to an emergency and lack of mental education, you were able to enter into the concentration form of operating. The result is notorious and, if you observe it, you will discover the power of a concentrated mind: you are able to introduce to your understanding one year of studies in a just few hours.

The same happens, for example, when we read a book; if you do it in the way of operating of the dispersed mind, it takes us years to do it and we might never finish– but it will indeed fulfill its function of being an eternal decorative object on your nightstand -; if we read it in the mode of gathering mental waves, it will take us some time, but we will succeed; if we read it in the mode of concentration, we might read the whole book within a few days. Read the book in concentration; you look at the clock and realize that fifteen minutes went by. Read the book in dispersion; you look at the clock, you discover that two hours went by and we are still on the same page!

Perhaps, time does not behave linearly and, although the clock's hands progress at a constant rhythm, what we can do, feel, know, and experience within ten minutes, changes notably according to the form of operating in which the mind is acting and receiving during those ten minutes. To a mind in agitation or dispersion, the ten minutes will pass quickly and probably does not do nor learn anything during that time; a concentrated mind can do and learn many things during those ten minutes.

Another useful example to understand how concentration works is that of putting a magnifying glass under the sun. Thanks to the concave angle of the crystal, the lens concentrates the sun beams, and if the union of its beams focuses on a point, it heats it up until the instance of creating a fire (try it; you need a magnifying glass, a sunny day, and a piece of paper to burn). The concentrated mind functions as the magnifying glass under the sun, it concentrates all the mental waves into a single point, in the direction of our objective and, it creates fire!

All the successful colleagues I have met (I use the term successful referring to their achievement of something, later I will talk deeper about "success" and "failure"), coincide on mental concentration being the acting mode of the mind that they use when doing work. Those who do something and achieve it have often accessed this of mode operating. However, they do not know what they are doing, they do not know about the ways of operating of the mind and about concentration, but at some time be it for external or internal reasons, they trained on this mode and use it to fulfill their objectives. A concentrated mind, achieves.

A mind that is being educated will train itself in the forms of operating in order to achieve concentration every time that the situation requires it or its will indicates it. It will give useful application to its concentration and will achieve set goals. An uncontrolled mind, if it at some time enters concentration mode, will do it due to the emergency of the situation, it will do it without realizing it; it will use this operating mode without control (sometimes applying it to useless, obsessive, or harmful goals) and once fulfilled, it will return to its usual agitation or mental dispersion.

16. MENTAL ANNIHILATION

We arrive to the most advanced operating way of the mind. It is the only one that can appear after something as efficient as concentration. This is the state of mental annihilation: when the mind has been concentrated to such a degree that mental activity disappears. In this operating mode, the mental waves disappear from the subtle field – and if they still exist, they have moved to another dimension, one that is far more subtle than the mental and astral field -. This is the operative mode that occurs when the mind melts into the present, it is a mental state usually known as meditation (active as well as passive).

In order to arrive there, work needs to be done, it is not something that happens by itself. The mind that is trained progresses step by step through the operative modes; it comes out from mental agitation when it defines objectives; it advances from dispersion to joining mental waves when it starts to focus its attention towards that goal, in acting or receiving according to the choice that has been made; it achieves concentration after practice, organization and focused attention; and when one has worked persistently on concentration, mental annihilation occurs. And I say "occurs" because, unlike the other progressive modes, this is the only mode that is not created by itself. The most that we can do within a good mental training is achieving a sharp concentration and applying it excellently. The mental annihilation, the disappearance of mental waves, the silence: it all occurs at once. We have come so close to that state that, without us deciding for it and its own autonomy, it instantly dissolves all concentration and allows us to be our true selves. This is the operating state of the mind that melts into the present, that operative state of the mind that is a being in itself, in full acceptance, belonging to its essence without there being a thing that does not belong to it.

Those who achieve concentration can do everything they aim as an objective while living. Those who achieve mental annihilation discover the joy of being, of existing, the constant celebration of a present life. Meanwhile in concentration, it has been proven that wellbeing exists within, and enjoying it is possible; inside the annihilation, it stops being a possibility in order to be a constant.

There are two possible ways of meditation: active and passive. If you observe them, you will discover that both are looking for the mind to pass from the state of joining mental waves to total concentration, in order to, by itself, be absorbed by annihilation and all mental activity disappears. In passive meditation, we normally have to sit in asana, lay down or accommodate ourselves into another position; guiding us to focus our attention to the third eye, the breath, or some other part of the body. In joining mental waves together, it is asking us to maintain ourselves there and if any thought arises, just let it go and gently come back there (developing concentration), until we finally, - without controlling it- are able to access a meditative state (mental annihilation). In active meditation, they usually ask us to sing, dance, repeat a mantra and other similar activities (joining mental waves). It will help us maintain ourselves present by repeating these activities – and if we are distracted, we revert gently into (developing concentration) – until we finally access a meditative state (mental annihilation). As it can be seen, it is a process that is developed between the three operative modes of the mind that generate wellbeing.

This is one of the reasons why singing, dancing, practicing sexual intercourse, performing sports, practicing artistic disciplines or working on any other task calms the mind. It is because they act as a mean to lead us to mental annihilation, many times this operative mode functions without even us realizing it. On the other hand, when the mind is too uncontrolled, these activities are not able to silence it; because you focus your attention on the gaze of another or on criticizing yourselves; you sing or dance, without involving yourselves completely to the activity; your mind drifts elsewhere during sex; you speak and repeat thoughts while practicing sports, you work or perform your discipline artistically, and a good number of other things.

Did you notice that some people need to work because if they do not, they will feel despair? Have you seen that some need to be doing something because otherwise they will suffer? That some stop doing an activity and become mad? This is a sign of an uncontrolled mind that discovered its only way of calming down and reaching annihilation is to be constantly active; and if it stops being active, the mind returns to an agitated state, leading itself to unavoidable suffering. These people need to do whatever they can do, even if it is a harmful and monotonous job, to avoid releasing that uncontrolled mind. The educated and trained mind does not need such an excuse to discover annihilation, because it does it through a conscious will directed towards practice and training.

A mind in annihilation, as it is in a constant present, will feel again, will be able to see what happens inside of it and in the world. Actively or passively, the mind performing in annihilation is the one that will allow you to be you and abandon any drastic shift to fake personalities. This is the operative state of the most healthy and efficient mind.

17. CONTROLLED AND UNCONTROLLED MIND

The uncontrolled mind will wander between the different modes of operating according to external or internal stimuli: affections, emotions, reactions, urgencies, or a superior dominating will. If there are no stimuli making it move towards concentration or annihilation, it will be abandoned within agitation (suspecting, digging, putting a minimal amount of attention on each thing, generating problems, destabilizing the being) and in mental dispersion (setting unachievable goals because it is unable to gather its mental waves in any direction).

A trained and educated mind will exit agitation and dispersion, it will function by gathering its mental waves in order to achieve concentration when it has an objective and will practice concentration so that it may be found by annihilation when it does not have to be active or passive (giving or receiving something).

The mind that has done great training understands each of the forms of operation well and dominates them; it will live in annihilation except for when a goal is being set, then it will go into concentration to perform it efficiently. When the mind is focusing all of its waves with concentration in one direction and towards an objective, hunger and thirst disappears, there is no sleepiness; the feeling disappears. This is because the mind is in full activity, all of our being is concentrated on that act. On the other hand, when the mind is in annihilation, mental activity disappears completely and we are pure feeling. The right sleep is there. If we are hungry, we will nourish ourselves with just what we need in its exact amounts. If we need to move, we will do it with the grace of moving with the world, and a large list of etceteras. This happens because the mind is silenced and the being is feeling. It is then that this mind will make us use it excellently when we will need to put it into action (concentration) and to silence it excellently when it is not needed (annihilation). The first state will guide us to be pure head (thinking); the second, to be pure heart (feeling).

18. WORK TO BE DONE

So far, you have finished reading everything about the four parts and the operative state of the mind. There are four main parts: the unstable mind, the intellect, the subconscious and the ego. There are five parts of the operative mind: mental agitation, mental dispersion, joining mental waves, concentration and mental annihilation. The parts of the mind perform like independent islands interacting between them. The operative modes perform like a ladder where we progress step by step successfully.

To sum it up, the parts of the mind that have to be worked on are as follow:

- Unstable mind: allows doubt. Open up your observation skills in order to expand its world.
- Intellect: deciding. Once the doubt has been installed by the unstable mind, solve it in order to progress.
- Subconscious: to realize. Whatever it is, let it be. Observe yourself and recognize everything that is kept safe within.
- Ego: de-identify and expand. Once we recognize something in the subconscious, de-identify yourself from it in order to stop being a slave to that memory and expand by identifying ourselves with the unknown.

The operative state, in short, works like this:

- Mental agitation: set goals in order to progress towards dispersion.
- Mental dispersion: focus our attention on the goal in order to be able to progress to the state of joining mental waves.
- Joining mental waves: maintain our attention on the main objective in

order to progress towards concentration.
- Concentration: practice concentration on a chosen activity in order to be absorbed by annihilation.
- Mental annihilation: maintain ourselves in a state of full presence.

These are the basis. Not much will happen if it is not worked on and practiced often. No one can do it for us. The world is too used to a useless way of acting. We live in a world of pills: believing that something external can solve the internal. The work of self-knowledge does not function this way. The outside are reflections of what happens to us, it is our roadmap in discovering ourselves. But a pill cannot do the work of self-knowledge for us (and when I say pill, you can also substitute it for master degrees, courses, miracles, luck, and a huge list of other similar things). All this depends on oneself; discipline, regularity, perseverance, and patience are virtues to be cultivated in order to be able to work on ourselves. In order to be able to count on a trained mind, it will not be enough to read a book, it is necessary to bring that idea into experience: practice it, apply all the knowledge that is being absorbed. Thus, it will become the way to bring that intellectual knowledge towards a feeling that will help you understand the idea; embody it and become it. It is easy, but it being easy does not guarantee that you will do it. Therefore, if one percent of the people reading this book do it, we will achieve something great. It is necessary to know what we want, but not just wish, dare to do it and achieve it. As a friendly reminder, I can say that once you have started, the journey becomes much more comfortable; it is like riding a bike; easy for those who are already able to do it, but risky and difficult for those who have not dared just yet. And those who already know how to ride that bike, know that sometimes we fall over in order to learn how to keep our balance.

Curiosity is fundamental in making it possible. If there is curiosity, that functions as a mysterious compass on our path, our mind will be interested in knowing what is there. If there is interest, we will be able to search it. Once found, it will not be discovered just yet; because while you will possess it right in front of your eyes, you still will not see it just yet. Only until you feel it you will, then, discover it.

Those who maintain an uncontrolled mind build up false personalities, follow mandates that do not belong to them and will not be interested in what they do. As a result, they find themselves with no curiosity. There is no interest; and therefore, the mind will hardly concentrate on these activities and will fly uncontrollably through agitation and mental dispersion.

If you dare on fixing the unstable mind, the intellect, the subconscious and the ego, and train your operative state, you will discover the changes in the world in which you experience your life with: those useless jobs, the pointless studies, the toxic relationships, and those false personalities all built upon your essence will disappear, and what belongs to you begins to come to light. Perhaps, at the beginning you will feel dizzy; by changing your world, you experience a first moment of vertigo, until you dare to jump in your new world and progress toward the next stability. Don't let anything stop you, and if you dare to train the mind, keep on searching!

-
-
-
-
-
-
-

19. EXAMPLES

The following examples are just caricatures. They only function as examples in order to illustrate the parts of the mind and the forms of operating in a more practical way.

The serial killer sniper. It is someone who does not leave the limited ego, identified with a very rigid image of themself. They do not recognize what is held in the subconscious, they do not enter the unstable mind but have great development of their concentration. Someone who is able to achieve excellence in what they do, but does not often ask themself if what they do is useful or not, if they contribute something to themself and to the world or not. Someone who has progressed very efficiently in the forms of operating and has achieved concentration, but has not educated the parts of the mind. They then apply concentration to non-productive goals.

The musician who has not achieved showing their music. It is someone who has progressed in the recognition of what they have held in the subconscious, they dare to enter the unstable mind and work from creativity, maybe they can even de-identify themself from their ego in order to compose humanitarian songs and see another as an extension of themself. However, they have not developed the forms of operating of the mind, they have not progressed beyond dispersion and mental agitation. So, they remain in a state of dreaminess, imagining that they play, but they do not; they imagine themself playing for great audiences, but they lie on their bed without leaving their room. They want to do great things and save the world, but they wake up after midday, they do not succeed in applying their attention and remain dispersed.

The successful surreal painter. It is someone that makes a great work of recognition on what they have held in the subconscious, they access their unstable mind and allow themself to repeatedly go back there. Perhaps their ego does not work much and they develop the forms of operating very well, easily succeeding in focusing their attention where their intellect says to and developing concentration. They become a great and creative artist with a strong ability in concentration and power to access the unstable mind, without serving humanity. They only produce the artwork to serve themself.

The successful humanitarian servant. It is someone that recognizes what they have in their subconscious. They expand their ego removing definitions and limiting identifications. They work on developing their intellect and progresses efficiently through the forms of operating of the mind. They achieve concentration in order to apply it in their study and work and administers their time to serve and give something useful.

The guru. They are someone that recognizes all they have held in the subconscious; they expand and de-identify themself from each memory to the point of unifying their ego with that of the universe. They fearlessly accesses the unstable mind over and over in order to expand and open up possibilities, until they succeed in accessing sacred acceptance, where all options take form. They excellently develop the forms of operating of the mind until they succeed in secluding themself in annihilation and returning to concentration when having to execute some thought, emit some word, or do some physical act.

CHAPTER 3

MENTAL TRAINING

1. DEFINING OBJECTIVES

2. PRACTICING CONCENTRATION

3. DISCIPLINE, REGULARITY, PATIENCE, PERSEVERANCE

4. PRESENT

5. MEDITATIVE MIND

6. SILENCE

7. ONE TRUTH

1. DEFINING OBJECTIVES

Defining objectives is one of the first activities that we must do in order to train the mind. As we have seen, the unstable mind will be the one that opens options, the ego will identify itself with some of them, the subconscious will paint them using our memories, and the intellect will decide which objective we will move towards. Defining objectives will give us a direction, an orientation, it will stabilize our course. It will help in training the ways of operating the mind, it will eliminate worries, and will even be capable, by giving us a purpose, of helping us come back to the present and to use it with a prior cause.

It is all about defining objectives for the day, the week, the month, for the whole year, objectives for the next five years, objectives for the next twenty years, and so on. There is no inconvenience with changing them on the road; if all the matter through which we experience the world through changes permanently, our objectives also can. If you train the mind you will discover that superficial objectives will vanish bit by bit –sometimes on the way, sometimes after achieving them- while the objectives that remain will be the essential ones in our lives.

A small target will, almost instantly, help us establish our future wanderings. For example, by correctly writing this paragraph I am working on and by being able to express the idea clearly and simply. This would be the objective that I establish for myself almost instantly when writing these lines. It is then that the mind will organize the knowledge it has on these matters in order to go towards the direction to accomplish this objective. Simultaneously, I establish another objective: write this chapter correctly, express every single idea with simplicity and clarity. It is then that I not only focus on this paragraph but I also, in the case of lifting my sight a little beyond the present, realize that I know where I am going, I have an established goal. It is then when the mind guides me to write these lines and every now and then I will lift my sight to discover how much I have deviated from the direction towards that chapter's purpose. Here, change also takes place. I do not stay rigid, hooked by this effort, but I allow myself flexibility. If I deviate in the path to that objective, as long as I keep doing this work, I let it happen so that I can see where my mind wants to take me (like a combination of consciousness and unconsciousness). Perhaps it conducts me into not only writing what I established for myself as a goal, but also features and comments that I did not consider in the beginning but become as useful as those I did (sometimes even more). If I lift my head a little further than my present and look into the coming days, weeks, and months, I will discover that there is also a determined objective: writing a book about the mind that is clear, simple, and false enough to become useful without creating attachment. I see where I am going, what my objective is with this book, and I return to lowering my sight to what I am doing in this instant, in the present.

An uncontrolled mind will not have set objectives, it will drift away, despairing, responding to stimuli without knowing where it comes from, where it is, and where it goes. A mind that is a little less uncontrolled, but still uncontrolled, may dare to establish objectives, however it falls into despair because it sees where it wants to go, it does not lower its sight to the present, it sticks to the future, sees it as unreachable, and falls into despair. As a response to that, it stumbles on everything ahead (because it does not see where it goes, it is entertained by fantasizing about the future), or becomes desperate because it can see the objective and does not know how to achieve it. It wants the object of desire and does not take that desire to do something now with its potential. It feels that it is difficult because it sees far ahead and cannot see what is here; it begins to write the line and gives up after two days because it keeps fixing its sights on the future, it does not savor the delights of writing what it must write now.

As it defines objectives, the mind stops wandering aimlessly with no course; it will abandon the mental state of agitation to go towards one of the mind's forms of operating with an objective –from mental dispersion to mental annihilation-. The difference, the way the mind operates from now on will depend exclusively on the work and training done. If there is one poorly done job, the only thing that it will reach is mental dispersion; there will continue to be trouble but at least it will not permanently be in the uncontrolled and chaotic activity of mental agitation. If we move forward a little, well-being will arise, which can be reached through gathering mental waves, achieving focus, or reaching annihilation. Once the objectives have been defined, the mind will begin to use time efficiently, in order to organize and define directions and work with what is presented to accomplish those purposes. It will no longer divagate like before, it will now have goals to achieve.

Establishing an objective consists of defining a point from where one is going to move towards, then one returns to their present to organize and work taking directions. Sometimes you make it, sometimes you do not, sometimes some other thing is achieved that was not necessarily the objective established from the beginning. Everything is worth something and everything is good. The importance behind the activity was never the goal itself, but the work that was executed to achieve it. Achieving is the job done, achievement is the result. One establishes an objective, works to accomplish it, and then sees if that achievement is the one that was established or another. The job is done and that is healthy; for us and everything that composes us.

It is also important to differentiate between objectives and expectations. They are not the same. Expectations are mental images, fantasies that have to do with how we imagine ourselves in a certain situation. An uncontrolled mind will attach itself with these projections and, thanks to that, will guarantee future frustrations and dissatisfaction –now that things never happen the way we imagine it-. If someone would like to achieve something just as they imagined it, they should have a will sufficiently strong enough to influence not only the will of all people on the planet, but also that of all the stars in the universe.

Objectives have nothing to do with expectations. While expectations are mental images, objectives are points that offer us a direction. They are as useful as points in the distance in which a sailor must focus their attention when they are sick in a boat, in the middle of the ocean, in order to recover from that state. Defining an objective is simpler than creating a castle in the sky (expectations); it is choosing towards where one wants to go and after that, by using the mind, we will distract ourselves with seeing how and with whom we want to go, and we will go on doing it.

Additionally, as we define objectives we are sending orders to the universe, consequently, to our life. There will be a cause and a purpose behind our wandering; The mind is going to use its powers on a channel. Every form of action that we perform will go in that direction, both consciously and unconsciously. From now on we will give ourselves path and there will be a purpose behind every thought, word, and action we make.

2. FOCUS TRAINING

Concentration is the fundamental practice of mental control. Once concentration is accomplished, it will be easy to reach this state several more times. The mind that concentrates on each activity it must complete gives their strength to that activity, it doubles the time, it extends the environment, focuses its potency, and makes a miracle arise. A mind in concentration does not waste vital energy, does not become distracted and offers the best of itself and positions one's being in one direction. Furthermore, as the mind is concentrated, hidden characteristics of the path reveal themselves.

In order to advance from mental agitation and dispersion, it takes making decisions and establishing objectives. The way to leave mental dispersion and enter the first state where there is mental wellbeing (gathering mental waves), one should place their focus on the objective. In order to advance from the form of operating that consists of gathering mental waves and reaching concentration, it is necessary to maintain focus on the objective.

The practice is simple. For example, let us say that the objective will be reading this book. Start reading it and you will discover that at some point you will become distracted and begin to do something else. An instant of self-observation will be enough to notice that you have deviated, and you focus back on the reading. Keep reading. If you become distracted again, focus on the reading again, keep reading. You will become distracted once again and again and you will focus one more time on the reading. Keep reading. Every time you go, come back. Gently, without fighting yourself, keep reading. This training consists in defining an objective, focusing on it every time you become distracted. You will discover that the first time that you deviated and returned to focus on the objective, you were distracted for fifteen minutes. The second time, ten minutes. The third time, five minutes. The fourth time, only two. And so on, until you suddenly realize that you have been distracted for only ten seconds. Continue. Suddenly, you will find that you can maintain focus on the activity you are doing and that if you become distracted, in an instant you will notice and will smoothly place your attention back on the activity. By repeating this practice, you will go on developing the power of concentration. After numerous repetition, you will find that you can easily master this activity and that you have achieved concentration for long periods of time without distraction; and in the case that you do, it will only be for an instant, a particle of a second, and you will quickly place your attention back on the activity and concentrate on it again.

In case that you do not have enough will and that it is hard for you to focus on the same activity, it is recommended to change your environment. Seek a different environment from the usual, where there are no stimuli that take your attention from what you are doing. Or pick an environment where other people are doing the same activity since it will positively influence the work of concentration.

You will reach concentration the same way that you achieved to learn how to read, write, walk, drive, use a keyboard, a computer, a bike: by practicing. As you practice, you will improve. As you practice, you will progress. If you become distracted, come back. If you cannot do it any longer, do not fight yourself, get away, take distance, and when you feel relaxed again, come back to the activity to continue practicing concentration. You will do it until you realize that in one moment you are in complete focus, and if a distraction appears, it will only be like a soft breeze: it will pass, it will touch you, and it will not affect you. It will pass, and you will continue in concentration.

You can practice concentration with the activity you want. It is preferable that we do it with something we like. As we go on achieving it, you will discover the results of the activity being done, revealing things that we did not see before. Through concentration, we can achieve and execute any objective that we propose to ourselves.

3. DISCIPLINE, REGULARITY, PATIENCE, PERSEVERATION

"80% of success is showing up." Woody Allen.

This phrase was once said by no one but Woody Allen. This man, who is considered a genius in what he does and has directed over forty movies, does not tell us that success is due to a stroke of luck, some divine chance, an extraordinary talent, some unique talent. No. He says that it is due, mostly, to the perseverance in what we do. He has spoken of perseverance as the greatest way to achieve.

Just observe someone that has achieved great development in any activity. If you look carefully, you will discover not only a frequent use of concentration, but also discipline perseverance and regularity (and patience comes as the cherry on the dessert, a possibility to do this work with harmony and without desperation).

Let us use the example of someone that will develop great musical abilities with the piano.

They begin from zero, at pure brutality; hits the keys of the piano, works with primi-

tive sounds, they know nothing about notes, scales, harmonies, melodies, rhythm, even less the technique needed to put the fingers on the keys; they only allow themselves to be led by the primitive instinct of sounds that are almost shamanic, they hit some keys, then others, maybe they will find a rhythm they like and maintain it. They continue to practice. After a while of practicing, they recognize some sounds, the way to sit in front of the piano has also changed, how they put their fingers on the keys; now their relationship with the piano seems more like a harmonic dance and not so savage. They keep practicing. Maybe they will be invited to join a band, now they have to play some notes for each one of the songs; they practice at home and the repeated attempts are now automatized and can be executed at recitals. They continue practicing . Maybe now they think of including alterations: changing some notes they had planned for the songs, because they like these sounds better—they become more familiar with the sounds-. They continue practicing . They are invited to play some songs with another band. When they go to rehearsal, they find that it does not cost much to learn the songs; even further, by listening to what they are playing, they start getting in tune with the other players, harmonically. They continue practicing. Now they realize they can play any melody they are shown in just a few minutes; the programming has accessed the body and recognizes the sounds; their fingers know where to go without the mind giving orders. They keep practicing. One day a little girl starts singing a song that the musician does not know, and advises that, by the sound of her voice, they can accompany her with the piano. They continue practicing. A friend arrives at their home and knocks on the door, the musician goes to the piano and knows what note sounds like that knock; the friend claps, and they know what other note sounds like the applause. Now the musician is developing such agile and precise physical intelligence, that they would know how to translate any sound that thy may listen to through the piano.

It was a story, an example of what someone that works with their concentration for a prolonged period of time would be, by practicing regularly with discipline, perseverance, and patience. This musician not only understood what was being studied, but also achieved feeling it; and as they felt each new knowledge, he had the capacity to execute them with precision. He no longer only knows about music, but feels the music and is capable of making it.

In its primitive state, little educated and unstable (at least until it is educated), the mind will hate and reject discipline, regularity, patience, and perseverance. The mind still uncontrolled will be hyper-volatile, always changing, it will jump from stimulus to stimulus, seeking for immediate results. It will get bored quickly, tending to laziness and corporal inaction (all activity of the being would be reserved for the mental internal dialog). On the contrary, the trained mind will achieve a state of concentration, possibly until annihilation, will know that discipline, regularity, patience, and perseverance are especially useful tools for the work done with itself. It is then that it will work to create, develop, and maintain them. These are trails that will lead the mind to organize and select directions more efficiently to accomplish stablished objectives.

It is worth pointing out that behind all this, there is something simple and specific: Living happily. How does one live happily? Stop looking for happiness on the outside and find it on the inside. How can it be found on the inside? By living in the full present, tasting everything that happens with all our senses without judging. How does one live in the present? By training the mind to work in the forms of operating of mental annihilation and concentration. How can mental annihilation and focus be reached? By consciously choosing to train to achieve it. How can it be achieved? By working each part of the mind and their forms of operating. How do they work? By knowing what they are, what they are for, what their abilities are, their advantages and disadvantages, and how to train them.

Very powerful things happen when you apply mental work with patience, perseverance, discipline, and regularity. And not only do you know this, but you are familiar with it. You have been doing it since you were born and when the programming enters your body, you forget them; nevertheless you are living through vital experiences on this field. For example, walking; once, it was an impossible mission however, the persevered practice has made them able to know how to walk. For example, swimming, riding a bike, driving a car, writing, talking, reading, among others. These are practices that need to be done with patience, perseverance, discipline, and regularity so they can be incorporated with us (and how you achieved it is forgotten). In the same way, one can achieve this autohypnosis, this programming, in any activity. How it happens is magnificent.

The mind yet uncontrolled will only train according to external stimuli, urgencies, and needs (how it moves, writes, walks, etc.); while a mind that trains itself and works on its education can go beyond these stimuli, urgencies, and needs, defining objectives and accomplishing them through practice with patience, perseverance, discipline, and regularity. This mind will turn any obstacle into an opportunity, will be able to endure, confront, and overcome any situation and achieve everything.

4. PRESENT

The mind's ways of operating are always focused back and forth, towards future and past: projecting, imagining, with expectations, defining objectives, remembering, memorizing, and repeating. The mind works on the temporal space. The mind cannot act in present tense. Maybe this will make us comprehend that there are things that the mind cannot understand: it cannot understand love, and it cannot understand the present, mystery, god, the infinite.

This is why I do not regularly talk about god, I do not speak of the truth; it is something far too large: reality. I know that speaking of it will be my failure, if I speak about something permanent through the impermanent I would be lying. The essence is something permanent. We can get close to it, with a trained mind, we can bring ourselves up to the door of essence, but to enter, something beyond our control is needed. I cannot define something permanent by using ephemeral words, if I do so, I would be lying. This terrain is too large. The mind does not understand it, it does not understand the infinite, it does not understand mystery, love, the present, god. Knowing that the mind cannot reach everything calms us. Maybe we can see that not all solutions are necessarily mental. Maybe there are solutions that pass through other centers or by mystery. The mind is good for some things, for others it is not.

The present is the time where everything happens and it is the place where everything is. Living in the present will make possible that we can feel again and be able to perceive what happens around us. The best that we can give of ourselves at all times is the here (and now). The present is where the mind goes mute because it works in a temporal space: between a past we remember and a future we imagine, or an imagined past and a remembered future. The mind in annihilation will be working in complete present.

Everything that happens to us is already in the past; while I am writing these lines, as they appear on paper, have already stopped being now and become a part of the past. On another side, the future will always be unknown and is impossible to predict. The unexpected will always come and the expected not necessarily.

The now, the present, cannot be held. It works as a bridge, a link, a tie between what will be and what was. What it is, the being, is only here. The mind works the same way; it is the bridge between the non-manifested and the manifested, between our essence and ourselves, between body and soul.

The now, the present, includes everything we need to evolve. If we have established an objective and the mind is working to go towards it, everything we need to do lies in the now. Does that mean that the achievement is in the present? Yes and no. The result is not there, but everything needed in that instant to take the necessary step on the path to achieve that result is. A mind completely in the present can achieve anything; if we have stablished an objective and we train ourselves to act from annihilation and mental concentration, it will allow us to see what the present provides for us to carry out what we are looking for, organize the present and take it as useful to do what it does in the best way possible. Completing one step, it instantly advances to the next, the coming present, which will introduce to us what the new situation requires to organize, make decisions, and do for the next step in the best way possible.

While you are there, you will see how everything dances around you. You will be able to feel. If the mind is in another place while you are here, you will miss out on many things (what is known as «being absent»). This is why some people can be more present in a situation without finding themselves physically there, while others find themselves there physically and may be less present. If the mind is elsewhere, entertained with opinions, definitions, and judging or expounding points of view, it will miss out on many things that are happening at the time. How many times have you absently read a few pages and when you realized it, you did not remember or know a thing about you read? Then you must go back on your steps to reread what was read a moment ago, but this time present, with your attention on the text.

A mind that is still uncontrolled is capable of identifying itself with its own points of views and opinions, solidifying them, and seeing the world through this mental helmet. This way, it limits itself and avoids living in the present. A mind that does not limit itself can be here (present) and not there all the time (future and past); it observes everything that occurs clearly, it will give the best use to its present and will make itself capable of enjoying it and organizing everything there is to go where it wants to go.

Another quality of the present is its connection to the body. The only way to feel the body is in the present state. When the mind is in annihilation, it can feel, and as it feels it knows how every organ in the body is, it will reconnect with itself and will know what it needs. A mind in annihilation will dialog in the same language with the body. An uncontrolled mind will be disconnected from the body and will not feel it. As we are present, we will know what will do us good in this present and what will not, what is useful and what is not. When absent, we can absorb what is useless as well as useful, without knowing, because we are in the head and we are not feeling. Can you remember what happened when you got hurt? If the mind was absent, it did not feel the hit; the moment in which you were present, the pain appeared.

Everything built will be done from here. Everything is done from here. We advance towards a constant becoming, in a chain of present times: present after present after present after present. It is also how animals work. They work in the immediate present, checking the environment with full focus, without paying attention to what others think of it: They will be here and now from the instinctive in a constant way.

Try to act like an animal for a period of time; enter a room and be as an animal that enters a space for the first time; everything is new, be sharp, smell, observe, hear, feel.

Another great activity to see what happens when we are in the present is to ask ourselves if we are breathing. Am I breathing? If you ask yourself that, in order to answer it, you will have to focus on breathing. In that moment you focus on breathing, to answer the question, you cannot think elsewhere and you cannot speculate mentally. And then you go back to feeling.

Two young people find themselves sitting on the sand, looking ahead towards the sea. One contemplates the beauty of the landscape. The other is waiting for the first to leave so he can get into the water and drown.

The first was present in the situation, contemplating the greatness of the ocean that they had before them. The second was far from the present, tucked inside his mind, traveling between the past and the future, trapped by his thoughts, considering suicide.

I imagine a great cavern and two doors located at two extremes of an infinite abyss. There is nothing that connects them and I am standing at one of the two doors, wanting to cross to the other. It is then that I imagine that I can build a bridge, but not all at once, but I build as I walk on it. The abyss remains, but I stop being so focused on it. I focus my attention on organizing the present as well as possible, to build the section of the bridge I am walking on. I build only as far as my foot can reach, and then I build again as far as my other foot can. I build a little more, and then some more, and step by step I am building the bridge. If I look forward, I can only see a huge abyss; full of despair, concerns, unresolved doubts, exaggerated fears, future problems; however, if I lower my head again and look at what is here (in the present), everything is very good. I give the best here, in this step, in this instant, where everything is clear and nothing is vague. I build the strength into the ground so that I can move onto the next step. I do not have to worry about what has yet to come, I occupy myself with what is here; I do not have to preoccupy myself with what is not there, I occupy myself with what is there. Focused on each present moment when I build the bridge, step by step, until I reach the door that is at the other side of the abyss.

I visualize myself at the feet of a giant castle; marvelous and spectacular, a human work and yet not so human. Everyone around me observes it in a state of shock, deeply affected by the greatness of this enormous and beautiful castle. For a moment I am also bewildered by its immensity, however, in the next instant, I lower my sight and observe a stone at its base, on the floor. After contemplating it for a few moments, I turn, I see a huge field that is behind me and discover a rock at the base of a tree, similar to the one at the base of the castle. Then I realize that the entire importance of the castle is there, in the same stone at the base of the tree; a simple, beautiful, and perfect stone. I realize that it is about the stones, placed one over the other, organized in a series of presents, of becomings, that made of precious loose stones a precious unified castle.

5. MEDITATIVE MIND

Mental annihilation is reached through concentration. Concentration is achieved by gathering mental waves, precisely, in a consistent way -- with discipline, regularity, patience, and perseverance in one point. Gathering mental waves is achieved through strong willpower, and obtaining a strong will is achieved through a worked-on and enhanced intellect. A great intellect is achieved through work done on the four parts of the mind. You then work on these parts of the mind by your own knowledge and superior will.

The concentration needed to reach mental annihilation can be carried out actively or passively. It is not something that is done physically, but a state in which we are absorbed spiritually. In order for this to happen, it is necessary to become sufficiently close enough so that the strength of the polarities can do the work itself.

The forms towards getting closer can be done through diverse ways: through concentration (on any activity we perform), through repetition of a mantra (active meditation), passive meditation (focusing silently on something), chanting, sex, going for a walk, focusing your attention on your breathing and body motion can work as tools to calm ourselves and get closer to this healthy state of mind.

In summary:

• By defining the objectives, we pass from mental agitation to mental dispersion.

- By paying close attention, you can go from mental dispersion to mental wave gathering.

- From gathering mental waves to concentration, sustain your focus and have it applied on one spot for a prolonged time.

From concentration to mental annihilation, maintain focused on the same spot for a prolonged lapse of time.

-

-

-

Mantras

The mantra is the verbal repetition of a word or phrase, at times it is significant, but not necessarily. The term mantra means «free the mind». It is conformed by two words in Sanskrit: manaḥ which means «mind», and trāiate, which means «liberation». It works as the repetition of a significant phrase —which could be any phrase— that keeps us here physically, because when we are repeating a phrase, what happens is that while thinking, we can end up somewhere else other than here.

While you are repeating the mantra, if you look at yourself, you are not thinking. You cannot be projecting, imagining, fantasizing, or whatever abrupt alteration that occurs from an uncontrolled mind. Repeating the mantra allows us to come back to ourselves, where we are found. The repetition of the mantra takes us to the now, the time and space in which everything happens.

The best way is through experimentation. Right now, do it. Choose any word and start repeating it. While you are repeating it try to think of something. Do you see what happens? There is no single thought. You can try to think, you can assimilate what you are thinking, you can pretend that you are thinking, but you are not. What happens when you repeat the mantra is that the mind, that was previously separated from the body, comes back to join it. This mental body, that was traveling through time and space, comes back to the now. And it is in this present that it joins the other mental bodies, aligning itself and feeling once more.

The repetition of a mantra compels the being to come back here, to the present, and when we are here, we come back to feel. When feeling, one reconnects with oneself (the selves that were separated join together into only oneself) and discovers what one perceives, needs, desires, and what is happening. The mind is elsewhere, thinking in the time plane, the body does not realize whether it is starving or not, it devours by programming; it does not realize whether it is thirsty, it does not realize if it is cold, and it cannot see anything that is currently happening. Until the moment in which the mind sets into the present; then it will come back to see and perceive. When the attention is outside the body, it does not perceive; when it is within it does. Imagine the number of imbalances that can occur for spending too much time on the outside, outside oneself, without feeling.

If you go to a Krishna temple you will find the importance that is adjudicated to the mantra. They know that the repetition of a mantra can conduct them to very high levels of consciousness. They spend most of the day repeating mantras, chanting and celebrating (while repeating the mantra), cooking (while repeating the mantra), doing temple chores (still repeating the mantra), like the bhaktis yogis. They know the power of the repetition of the mantra.

When picking a word or phrase for the mantra, it is helpful to remember that each word has thousands of years of history in which they were formed and built upon. Each word has an extensive history, that is why affirmations are very powerful and useful to focus on. Anything we say (its construction, its origin, its composition) entails an extensive history.

Of course, there are words that are felt more than others, according to the vital experience that each person has had. That is why it is more meaningful to pick a word that represents something that raises us up, or a phrase, such as a mantra, than saying just whatever. However, all of them work to accomplish the objective and reach mental annihilation and get back to the present.

A focused mind will construct to us anything we desire, it will achieve any objective we give it. The mind drives us crazy if it is not under control; because it always wants to act, always wanting more. That is why it needs activities and tasks, or any activity (such as a mantra) that quiets and entertains the mind.

Any phrase is sacred. You don't need to travel to India, do Diksha, shave your head, have someone to tell you what your mantra should be in a language you do not understand and repeat it without feeling it. A mantra can be a repeated «Thank you», or a «Mom's coffee maker reminds me of the scents of my childhood» or «Tomato soup». Anything counts. It can be any word or phrase that is repeated with discipline and perseverance. If the phrase brings us to a memory or a feeling that gives us pleasure, then it is twice as powerful. The same can happen if the phrase influences us positively; These could be mantras such as «thankful for life», «Freedom», «I am beautiful», etc. Therefore, the word or words that are used not only will work as a mantras but can also autosuggest us. It is then that the selection of a meaningful word or phrase that has a positive or neutral resonance in ourselves will be twice as useful; it will conduct us to mental annihilation, and it will stimulate us.

Meditation

«Meditation is the result of the practice of concentration. It shows clearly what we have within our minds, which are the subjects we get entertained on, and which are our psychological tendencies. It helps us to de-identify from those tendencies and have a bigger control of power over the mind, it opens the soul, the spirit, develops judgement and intuition, and brings peace, serenity and fullness».[3]

Meditation, whether it is active or passive, takes us to a state of full presence and leads us up to a state of mental annihilation. It is the work needed to reach this internal state. As we approach, we discover that there is a certain clinging to the mind which is not allowing itself to release; things

---

[3] Lou Couture and Leandro Taub, Homemade Wisdom

that are entertaining the mind, which are its psychological tendencies, that have guarded the subconscious without being recognized and what is the foundation of our profoundness. The practice of meditation helps us to de-identify ourselves and take a step back, making the problems that seem like big tragedies look nothing more than a funny anecdote.

Active meditation is the result of a task that gets done in a repetitive way during a determined lapse of time until the mind reaches the annihilation. The mantra is a type of active meditation. Any activity that moves the mind from its imaginary work and make it focus until disappearing is an active meditation: singing, running, swimming, dancing, breathing repeatedly, and a great number of other things.

On the other hand, passive meditation comes through inactivity, through not doing. This type of meditation is the most complicated because it applies such a skilled management of intellect so our will can be controlled to avoid authorizing the mind to entertain itself with thoughts, letting go every emotion and idea that come as a wave that arises and disappears. This type of meditation is usually practiced by placing the body in an asana position and focusing your attention towards the third eye, in breathing, in another part of the body, and among other forms: you fix your attention to a point and then, you must be attentive enough to maintain concentration on it until it disappears when you become absorbed by the annihilation. In this type of meditation, one should not fight against what is coming; if thoughts come, they simply let themselves pass, without letting it entertain us. We can observe how they come and go, without stopping there.

Breathing

The breath is our first support of life. We can breathe both voluntarily and involuntarily. We can pay attention to the way we breathe, direct it, choose how we do it and educate it; we can also not pay attention to the way we breathe and do it involuntarily, unconsciously, in a mechanical way. The difference between the two activities is a great stretch. Automatic breathing will give us a small sip of air, the minimum necessary to sustain the great machine of the body. Voluntary breathing that works well can give us a great daily supplement of wellbeing and health.

The breath works between our most subtle and densest field. It works between the mental body and the physical body. It works between ideas and emotions, desires and needs. It works between the mind and the heart, and the sex and the body.

When we are in an altered emotional state we breathe short, agitated breaths within our chest. When we are in a state of calmness, the breathing can become deep and we send air to the diaphragm. This is the breathing that calms us, it is the breath that babies do when they sleep; abdominal breathing. In a very agitated emotional state, our breathing will be short, within the chest. A single moment of attention is enough to realize how we are breathing and lower our breath to the abdomen: the emotional state will lower along with the breathing and we will calm down.

On the other hand, voluntary and conscious breathing offers another great tool: the control of the mind. When we place our attention on the breath, we cannot think of anything else.

A good breath heals. It brings us to the present. It forces us to come together (with ourselves) and feel. Most of the day we are working on our minds and not feeling. From the mind we are traveling through time, wasting great powers, without being here, without living what life is giving us.

«Life is what happens to you while you're busy making other plans.» John Lennon

In addition to working on our emotional states and reassuring ourselves, in addition to forcing ourselves to return to the present, in addition to silencing the mind, conscious breathing has another great advantage: it loads us with vital energy. The vital energy, prana or chi, is found everywhere and in our body. All the vital energy that we take comes from the sun. We take the most subtle vital energy through the air and the densest through food. Voluntary breathing can offer us larger puffs of vital energy in its subtle form of air.

Rhythmic Breathing

The rhythmic breathing also works as an efficient mantra or active meditation. It not only forces us to come back to the present but also charges us with vital energy.

Breathing can be performed consciously or unconsciously; it can be voluntary or involuntary. If we do it voluntarily, we will take more prana from the air, it will give us more energy than when we do it involuntarily. Therefore, even when we «spend» a lot of energy running in the woods, afterwards we feel more cheerful, with more strength and more energy... to achieve this rhythmic breathing, when we walk (instead of being lost in our minds) we can feel our breathing and put it together in our steps. Try to do a conscious breath with these steps: for example, inhale two times, exhale twice (each one adjusts their breathing with their steps): And while we are walking, feel it, be one with your breathing. Doing this is magical because it produces fast changes if we do this regularly.[4]

Rhythmic breathing does not only fill us with mental energy and give us life, but it also works as a mantra; if we focus on doing it consistently, it will bring us to the present, it will join our body, and make us come back to a state of touch. Try to breathe deeply, with your stomach –the breathing known as abdominal breathing-: while we walk, while waiting, while traveling in a car, while doing nothing, while doing something; repeat this breathing with focus. When practicing it, you will find not only that you are in the present, but also that you are feeling and seeing what is happening. You will stop walking across the street like a zombie –and you will discover a great number of "zombies" that walk through life hypnotized; walking on the street, working in their offices, relating to their families, making their lives absent, always thinking without paying attention to what happens around them, because they are entertained in remembering and protecting, in imagining, in suspecting, and in digging internally, in talking without seeing the world in which they live in and what is happening around them-. The importance of the mantra, whatever it is, is that it brings us to the present and

---

[4] Lou Couture and Leandro Taub, Homemade Wisdom

brings us here (in the now). Try repeating the name of a fruit that makes you remember something pretty; make up any word and repeat it; place your attention on breathing and count it; while you cook, while you work, while you drive, while you shower, or while you walk. You will realize the power of coming back to the present.

6. SILENCE

Silence is one of the most efficient tools for self-discovery. The average human being has thousands of thoughts a day, and we externalize many of them. Keeping silent, not externalizing everything that comes to mind, listening to ourselves, listening to our thoughts and actions and listening to our states, work as a form of effective self-observation that manifests frictions, contradictions, and affectations that we are not willing to recognize.

The practice known as «silence practice» consists of not speaking for an entire day to a whole week, and, if that is not possible, for at least half a day. During this practice we continue doing the activities in our schedules, but on this day they must be done without talking. This is a practice that is recommended to observe what level we are on when communicating with others, in which way we are relating to others, what kind of conversations do each one of the clans we involve ourselves in hold and which are the impulses that urge us —like a form for recognizing the memories anchored in our subconscious—.

On one side, the outside: you will see at what level you are dialoging with the world, at what level you relate to your friends, with your family, your partner, your work, your studies; you will see if the family chats about ideas, things, or other people. These are different types of conversations. It will also work for self-observation. Not being able to speak does not mean that you cannot think —unless you are in a state of full presence, an active and passive meditation wandering and going intermittent—. Unless you are already trained on that, you will think. When you are not externalizing your thoughts through actions or words, the only thing left for you to do is twist creating more and more a more thoughts or, begin to observe what you are thinking. You will have a very active mind. Then, you will be able to observe it. Usually, you are not observing it because you are externalizing it. Someone says something, the impulse to give an opinion will come, but you do not say anything. Then you can observe what you could have said. And you can measure it: Was what I was going to say productive? Was I giving someone something? Was it useful? Was it useless? Did it have something to do with an exposure of my vanity? Was I serving the other? You can observe everything you would say without saying it. This way you can constantly evaluate yourself and train the mind. You say without saying. You see how you would react. It is a great practice to recognize what you have within your subconscious. This is because the subconscious will act before the nerves (not muscular nerves but psychological). If someone were to tell us something that affects us, we would generally react to it. But if we are practicing silence, we do not react, then someone tells us something that affects us, touches our nerves, the reaction comes out, and then you observe what is coming and where it is coming from.

7. ONE TRUTH

I cannot tell you the Truth, I cannot explain it, and if I try to describe it, I would be lying. It is the one that guarantees that everything I say will be a lie. I cannot describe it, I cannot talk about it, the moment I try to name it, I will fail.

But here I will not be working with that one, I will be working with this one by speaking to you about the practice of the truth in another way. Here, we will speak about the truth as saying what we think and doing what we say. It is about the practice of congruence and reciprocation with the commands we send. Lining up our powers to potentiate ourselves. To respect one truth between the thought, the word, and the physical action we are performing. It means that what we think corresponds to what we say and what we do. When we pay attention to aligning these three things, each action we perform will be supported by the other two things. Then we potentiate ourselves. This way, each word, action, and thought becomes law. The need to insist, repeat, or stun disappears. When the three forms of action align, what we do makes us. What we do pushes the world. Also, it creates tranquility and calm, you stop wasting vital energy and focus on the activities you want to do. Also, it quiets unnecessary mental dialog.

How many of us say one thing and then do another? Or promise and then do something else? Or do something while we think another? Or say something while thinking about something else? Or say what you did not do or will not do? Then you later have to, unconsciously or consciously, cover lies. You waste your powers and confuse your path.

How many people go crazy because what they perceive is different from what they say? They have parents that do not love them in practice but tell them that they love them. Or have a partner that does not love them in practice but tells them that they love them.

The disciple approached his master, curious to know the secret of his great wisdom and capacity to do spectacular miracles. The master told him: «When I eat, I eat. When I speak, I speak. When I sleep, I sleep».

The practice of a truth —aligning the thought with the word and physical action— is a fundamental tool to the training of the mind. It additionally has a power behind of it, which is the network of chances that determine our constant becoming in life. Everything that happens to us is a result of our interaction with the universe. The way we interact occurs through the de-clothing of our souls; what we think, what we say, and what we do. Executing the practice of a truth helps us pay attention to the way we act, to correspond to ourselves and avoid the contradictions and frictions that trouble us. It will take awareness of what we are doing in its three forms. As a result of this activity, you will discover that nothing happens by chance, but that everything is part of a network of coincidence, that everything that happens is the result of actions we made before. The coincidences disappear, the synergies and coincidences become wider, and the world stops being seen as an accident after an accident and comes to be seen as the result of actions.

As additional results, paying attention to what we do, say, and think will erase concerns, stabilize the mind, and potentiate every action, besides economizing our vital energy. It will erase concerns, because if we have placed our attention on each thought, word and action, then we will give the best of ourselves in each one of our actions. We do it as best a possible in each one of the instants, it could not be done better (regret vanishes) and there is no other thing we can do but what we are doing in each one of those moments we apply attention to (concerns vanish). It will stabilize the mind because it stops confusing it with crossed commands, it stops contradicting itself when doing something and saying another thing, it will stop wasting time on covering lies, and the mind finds order. It will potentiate every action, because now each one of them will be supported by corresponding thoughts or words; now each thing that is done not only has the strength of the action per se, but it will also be joined by the thought and words that push it. It will economize vital energy, because now you are using it precisely on thinking, saying, and doing things that are useful and that correspond to each other; commotions caused by self-produced confusions stop occurring.

The best we can do for the other is the best we can do for ourselves. The best we can do for ourselves is practice the truth with ourselves.

CHAPTER 4

OPENING THE MIND

1. INFINITE POINTS OF VIEW
2. MENTAL SPACE
3. SELF OBSERVATION

1. INFINITE POINTS OF VIEW

There are many points of view from which to analyze each thing. The rigid points of view, with time, solidify more and more in our minds and limit us. We usually think from a rigid side when seeing things. What happens when we set a rigid point of view in the mind is that it solidifies (opinion, belief, ideas). As it solidifies, we do not see the total of what we could see. Then limits are created. We build walls that accompany us for years.

It is useful to play at changing the points of view. Although the idea seems clear, we must doubt, access the unstable mind to expand ourselves. Take an idea and taste it, see how far it can take you and what its limits are. Then taste another idea, see how far it can take you and what its limits are. With one more and with another, and with yet another. Try changing the points of view, contradicting ourselves, expanding ourselves, and leaving the false comfort.

2. MENTAL SPACE

Without self-annulation there is no possible learning. By offering space to the mind, possibilities open up. To give space to the mind it is necessary to release established knowledge, stop seeing the world through what we know and allow ourselves to do it through the unknown. Although intellect seeks to understand everything, we do not need to do so in order to expand our minds. Even more so, seeking to understand everything goes against expansion. Defining the unknown through the known will not make us discover the unknown. If we do not give the mind space, the new cannot enter. If we do not give the mind space, it will easily identify itself with the emotion or thought that appears at the moment. This space will offer us the possibility of letting go of identifications. If the mind finds itself gripped, giving it space will offer it the possibility of letting go and will offer other possibilities.

The unworked ego will be identified with the conditioning, mandates, customs, habits, opinions and ideas. It will remain very identified with those images in the subconscious. By giving space to the mind, the ego is offered the possibility of distancing itself a little from this identification and observing.

To give space to the mind is to take distance and it works toward closing stages. A hand that is holding something has no space to grab anything new. The same applies to the mind; you need to have permanent space to be able to expand and have the terrain to work on and continue with your training. When one takes distance, everything becomes small: problems, objects, stories, rivalries, differences; life itself. Looking from this perspective, "problems" cease to be. As we take distance and give space to the mind, it becomes less important to involve ourselves in something that is not useful.

Those who do not take distance define their essential being with the ephemeral emotion they are feeling and project it for all eternity. By offering yourself space you take distance, you discover that X emotion does not belong to you and that it accompanies you for as long as you decide to carry it. Everything passes. Emotions are transient, they last as long as identification with them lasts.

Taking distance offers us a larger image of the small circumstances with which we are identified. We do not usually watch the whole movie, but we see a small piece of a single scene. Giving the mind space and taking distance will not make us see the whole movie, but it will offer us a change of perspective.

It is all about taking distance to be able to observe. For example, if one climbs a mountain and sees a city from there, they will distinguish everyone moving as if they were ants. It changes the way they see things. The same thing happens when you travel by plane, when sailing at sea, or when observing the stars at night; the immensity of the universe is seen, the immensity of the film that we are experiencing. In doing so things change, distance is taken, life changes in magnitude.

If you accept the emotions as they are and honor them, they last a brief visit and pass. If they are taken and fed or rejected and fed; emotions are preserved and grow.

As we give space to the mind, it changes the level of relaxation and distance we have from the objects of affectation. As we give space to the mind, we can more easily de-identify memories and instincts housed in the subconscious. The big problems, the limits and solidifications occur when we identify ourselves rigorously and take hold of the idea. When we distance ourselves, we move away from this identification. We do not separate ourselves from the world, we instead separate from our little world. We do not separate ourselves from the other, we instead separate from what affects the 'us' that we see reflected in the other. Taking distance is to achieve the necessary space for the mind to separate itself from the ideas and emotions with which it is identified, it allows us to work with ourselves and improve ourselves.

As an example, look at the stars at night, look from the top of a mountain and see everyone walking like little ants, or stand in front of the sea and see the immensity of the ocean. When you take distance, everything looks small, even problems. If one comes much too agitated; give the mind space, it calms.

Some exercises to achieve this are:

- Putting the established knowledge aside to allow us to see other points of view.

- Retain the need to present our point view or opinions.

- See at least five distinct forms of each of the events.

- Do not identify with the first thought or emotion that comes to you.

- Listen to music.

- Think of the immense.

- Review great works, great stories, and great virtues.

- Read sacred books.

It does good for the mind to be fed with sublime things. Incorporate great things that elevate it: sacred books, nature, something that does not take your breath away and places it in a state beyond that of human conflict.

The best experimentation is with oneself and through the opposites we easily understand. Observe yourself and notice the difference between the different states: watch the news and then watch yourself; see how are you mentally and emotionally. The next day, at that same time, watch a program on nature, one that shows landscapes, biographical stories, or great works. Notice the difference, how you find yourself at a mental and emotional level.

3. SELF OBSERVATION

Self-observation is the great tool for the work of knowledge of one's self, for the mastery of the mind and work in mental training.

Let us begin with the following: while reading these letters, without taking your eyes off of them, pay attention to how you have your neck, how your legs are, what temperature the soles of your feet are at, how your stomach feels, pay attention to how your breathing is working. Can you do that? If you succeeded; what happened? Suddenly, there were two of you. There was the one that read these letters, this book; while there was also another you that was observing yourself and observing how you were performing this reading, how your body was, your organs and your breathing.

If there were two of you: who are you? Were one of you real and the other fake? Are both real? Are you many? Perhaps the 'you' reading these letters is the personality; it is the disguise of your essential being, the layers of personalities and forms acquired from birth to this moment. Perhaps the self that observed you while reading is your essential being or consciousness; the silent witness who can observe you.

This thing that you have just experienced is what is called unfolding. It is not that complicated, you just lived it in an instant. And if you want, you can practice it again now; without taking your eyes off the book, pay attention to how your stomach feels, your shoulders, your knees, your eyes, your lips, your sexuality, your emotions. Also try to do it while cooking, or while walking, or while lying down. Each time you decide to do so you can turn to that silent witness, who coexists with you to self-observe and see how you are at all levels.

This is the greatest tool, and the most powerful, for our work. The more we self-observe, the more we can see how we speak, how we think, how we act, what we speak, what we think, what we do; we can review how we feel, how our body feels, our emotions, our desires, and needs. Through self-observation you can remain vigilant and learn from yourselves. And not only that, you can also separate yourselves from the body and observe it; discovering that we are not just the body. We can separate ourselves from the mind and observe it, discovering that we are not only the mind and the body. And by taking distance from the mind and the body we can control and master them; stop acting as slaves to our bodies and our thoughts, and become their silent witness, who is capable of observing the situation from the outside and take control.

If you begin to perform this practice, you will experience an absolute change of life. Observe what you do and how you do it, observe what you think and how you think, observe what you say and how you say it. You will have control of yourself. By doing this you will move away from the thought and emotion reflex, to move to determined thoughts. By doing this you can easily discover your affectations and contradictions; you will be able to discover which are the memories and instincts stored in the subconscious; you can make distance, give the mind space and de-identify the ego.

Through self-observation you can discover and become surprised that maybe you are not being who you are: maybe you do not say what you want to say, maybe you do not do what you want to do, maybe you do not live the way you want to live. Through self-observation you can discover all the lies that you tell to yourself and how you present them to the world, looking for its acceptance and approval. Through self-observation you can discover if there is a false life that you are experiencing and what your essential being is asking you; you can discover its deepest desire and, if you dare, jump into its fulfillment. Through self-observation you can discover the definitions that you give to yourself and the world, the mental boundaries you build and, if you dare, you can strip them, crumble them, liberate yourself, expand yourself, and go on.

If you self-observe you may realize that you are forgetting yourselves. That you are working at a level of absolute attachment with every thought and emotion you experience, at every moment that passes, and in the next instant you forget what just happened and attach yourselves to the next thought and emotion. You will discover that you project this temporary identification towards infinity, believing that this emotion or thought will last forever, making life decisions according to temporary emotions and thoughts. You will discover that you act in response to the crazy ideas you have kept, that come out of yourselves, that you do not remember, that you ignore your essential being, that you ignore the other, that you do not observe, that you do not act according to what you need, desire, feel, or think, you instead advance like reactionary machines from accident to accident.

Sometimes we forget ourselves, we believe every emotion is eternal, and we act according to them.

Practicing self-observation, one discovers the essential being as well as the layers of the false self.

CHAPTER 5

ONESELF AND THE WORLD

1. THE RIGHT MEASURE
2. THE FAIR ACT
3. WHO DOES THE GIFT BELONG TO?
4. REFLECT EMOTIONS AND THOUGHTS
5. SELF-OBSERVATION EXERCISES
6. NOT TAKING THINGS PERSONALLY
7. THE OPINIONS
8. DIVERSITY

1. THE RIGHT MESURE

When using the cause-effect law (karma), if we feel and experience that everything that happens is a result of what we think, say and do, then, being fair to ourselves –and, therefore, to the world- would be the best we can do to face each circumstance.

Doing justice to ourselves is not about waiting for other to give us what we don't know how to give to ourselves. Who awaits the other to give, maybe is still under a maternal or paternal archetype; waiting to get food, home, shelter, love, to have everything served. Who has advanced a little more further from this situation discovers that we have what we give and that we build according to what we do. When we see a little further, we can stop waiting to get everything from the other and start from ourselves, to offer, to give ourselves.

There are many people waiting nowadays; they wait for everything to happen and they are in despair when nothing happens. They are waiting for a magic pill to resolve an illness, a magical method to dissipate their traumas, that a magical world do their job. It is useful to be giving ourselves what we deserve and not waiting the other to do it for us. This way we take what we need and take away what doesn't suit us, we take what we deserve and offer what we have.

2. THE FAIR ACT

The moment we actuate within the world, we can observe where the impulse is coming from. When I say «actuate», I refer again to physical acts, words and thoughts. It is useful to check each one of them and discover where they come from. It is not the same acting from unstable emotions tan from necessities, it is not the same acting from selfish desire than from situational requirements.

When we work with our minds, it is useful to act from the sense of duty, necessities, possibilities, the right thing, the fair thing and the requirements of the situation. The same way you check where you act from, it is useful to avoid acting from selfish desire, unstable emotions, and unconscious reactions and instinctive impulses.

Necessities have more to do with the physical plane, the desires with the sexual plane. Necessities are basic, food, shelter, home, health. The desire has to do with something that emanate. Desire can't be created. You can't create desire for the other. Neither can we erase it. It has to do with the instinctive and sexual of each one of us. What we can do is channeling it and focus it with the mind towards a purpose.

One knows it. After that, it is necessary to see the tricks we pull to ourselves. Before acting, if you observe, you can know where the impulse come from. It is useful to check where every one of our actions proceed from and ask ourselves if the situation requires us to act that way or if we are doing it for a different motive, something inside of us that needs to be resolved.

There is a great difference between acting according to what the situation demands and acting according to selfishness, unstable reactions or emotions. The difference between both actions is huge, it is about what we give to the world and our game with manifestation.

What is the best I can do for the other? It is the best I can do for me. By helping me I help the other. Everything I give to the other I give it to myself. Whatever is good for me I share. Denying the other? Suppress it?

3. WHO DOES THE GIFT BELONG TO?

If someone gives you something and you don't accept it, to whom does it belong?

They can offer you any gift, for example, a bag of insults and aggression. By not authorizing this aggression, by not taking this gift, it will continue to belong to the one who offered it. If you don't take it, it remains the other's problem. If you take it, you make it your problem. Is it useful to react? Is there something useful in reaction? What would happen if we reacted? Is it necessary to prove something?

If they give you something you don't accept, who does it belong to? There is an evil game in which someone carries negative energy and comes forward to give it to someone. While many react and follow the game, whoever that doesn't react gets protected. Is defending vanity reasonable? For an uncontrolled mind it would be. A controlled mind will act if the situation requires it; if a threat shows up or if it puts yours or the others' health at risk. If it is a verbal game, a vain activity, the controlled mind has no reasons to participate. A mind that is controlled will use the impulse of reaction, not to externalize it toward struggle, but as a tool to verify which nerve it touches; to recognize the saved memory in the subconscious and the ego identification. In this way you can take external aggression to work upon yourself, observing your darkness and discovering why this would have made you react. This way you would use your own reflection upon the other as a tool for self-observation and the discovery of your essential being.

Maybe this is the reason why there is a great gratitude for the so-called «enemies». The opponent, unlike someone who supports us, will be the one that stimulate us and help us, without even wanting to, to discover which are those frictions and inner contradictions that we haven't yet recognized. These «enemies» will provoke us in every single way, and if by any chance we feel affected, then it means that we have been granted a map with the precise sign of where one of the treasures for our self-awareness lies.

Compliments work this way, but inversely. When we believe the pretty nice things that someone comes to tell us, vanity could emerge. If vanity gets inflated, if our being identifies with a compliment, there will also be work to do. Many people can't see it: they just take the compliment, feed their vanity, strengthen their identification with these images and waste the opportunity that has been offered by the other to work on themselves. If you observe how your mood has changed and why, you will also find that there is ego identification over some subconscious memory that is useful to work upon: recognizing, de-identifying and letting go, to keep expanding ourselves toward a union with our all-inclusive divinity.

Instead, the uncontrolled mind will manifest its limits and unsolved inner conflicts. This way happens with people who attack or assault someone else. Why do they do it? Is there something hidden behind it? Maybe they are externalizing their own suffering, their inability to self observe and recognize what is happening to them, and as they can work with themselves, they will see it reflected as something that bothers them from the other person. If you don't do any kind of inner work you will believe that others are responsible of the suffering you carry and you will fight against the other, you will seek to provoke them, you will try to destroy them, with the objective of destroying your own suffering. If you put restrictions to yourself you will tend to externalize them and reflect them on others.

Perhaps, instead of externalizing your own limits, you can observe the impulse of what you are about to do or say, or just check the thoughts you are having. Behind all this, you can find what is demanding attention and review. Maybe, instead of externalizing, we can look through ourselves, take every impulse as an opportunity for self observation, and then, in order not to repress it or save it, you can express it through useful channeling. Not externalizing it toward others, inviting them to perverse games, but expressing it in a useful, creative or reproductive way for oneself.

4. REFLEX EMOTIONS AND THOUGHTS

«Every object, word and idea brings the mind a correspondent thought to this subject, an idea, a memory or an opinion is already established from long ago. Then, our response mechanism come from this point. Each time someone tells us about some subject we are going to answer with our correspondent preset thoughts. We often want to share this idea, transmit this correspondent thought, even when this is not necessary. In order not to get stocked in this automatic response behavior of always repeating the same about this subject (check also the practice of silence); on the other hand, we can try to amplify our responses about this word or idea that seeks for other memories, other sensations, and new ideas.»[5]

Reflex emotions and thoughts are impulsive reactions originated as a response mechanism toward a external stimulus that touches an inner nerve. We keep memories and instincts in our subconscious that our ego identifies with. When someone says or does something that resound with one of these identifications (when it touches an inner nerve), a reflex emotion or thought emerges as a response mechanism. Therefore, each time an impulse comes from a reaction – on thought, word or action basis- we have in front of us the opportunity to recognize something that we are seeing; a stimulus has been presented in front of us that touched a nerve. If we take

---

[5] Lou Couture and Leandro Taub, Homemade Wisdom

it as an opportunity, we can, instead of reacting, turn it around, explore our darkness and take that reactionary impulse as a lantern to see which memory is stocked in our subconscious, seeking to be recognized. This is the programming that comes to light. It is expressed as a defense or fighting mechanism. Instead of reacting, we can observe.

5. SELF-OBSERVATION EXERCISES

Some of the tools we can use to improve self-observation, discover what we keep in our subconscious and recognize it, are:

- Observing repetitions. Everything we repeat (words, thoughts, actions in the form of habits) correspond to an inner programming. Everyday is unique; the same way should happen with thoughts, words and actions. If this was to happen, it's because a programming that is settled in our subconscious is operating, which is also something that the ego identifies with. Checking if there is any repetition in our behavior and way of acting in this world will be useful to see what we repeat, why we are doing it and what is that pattern telling us.

- Practicing silence. A few chapters before, when we were talking about silence, it was underlined that it could be useful to remain silent and then observe what we would have said. Then we would be self-observing. We will be able to see which are the reactions we have even before reacting; what are the impulses that invade us in the form of actions, words or thoughts; we will discover the reflex emotions and thoughts, and then we will be able to see which are the nerves that have been affected; it will provide a map to discover other memories that we keep in our subconscious and that our ego identifies with.

- Pausing before answering. Instead of reacting to an external stimulus, it is useful to make a pause before answering. This pause will be useful to check if what we are going to say or do have any purpose, if we are offering something valuable to others or not. It is useful to discover the source of what we are going to say, the motive of what impulses us and the objective it is seeking.

• Speaking slowly. If we change the rhythm of our dialog, we will be able top pay more attention to each word we say; not only the word itself, but also the way we say it. If we speak slowly, we will have the chance to self-observe while we speak. Then, we will be able to check while we are acting.

• Amplifying our response field. This is very useful to come out of solidified programming. As we amplify our response field, we are granting the unstable mind access and changing our world; we open possibilities and if we act using our intellect to make decisions, we are offered the opportunity to expand while we act in this world. Widening the field of our responses, expands us.

6. NOT TAKING THINGS PERSONALLY

It is not about the messenger, neither about de message, but about what resounds within ourselves and gets projected in the part of the message we are listening to. There are people who create a huge story out of anything they listen to; they believe that everything that is said is directed to them, even what they read, what they hear on the streets, on the TV, newspapers, an alien talk; everything resounds to them, everything is seen as a sign. Which is, in a sense, false and yet real. It would be false to interpret a message literally and believing that the world spins around us, and things are like other people say so; in this case the massage we are receiving from others will affect us, causing us to react according to it, modifying our behavior according to the point of view or opinion we get from others, constructing layers and layers of disguises on the essential being, covering it up with fake identities and personalities, built by strange impressions, strange examples. This would mean that we are acting according to what others say (in order to be loved, believing that we are what we are and not what others want us to be, we wouldn't have the right to receive love). It would be real, if we didn't take the message literally, but as a sign to self-observe, realizing that our mind allows us to hear exactly what we want to hear, not to take it as a literal sign, but to help us discover what is hidden within this matter. Behind every message that resounds to us, there is a sign that we have to listen to, in order to discover ourselves.

If we don't work on ourselves we will react by getting angry or happy with the Messenger. In this case, whoever says something that bothers someone will be condemned. This condemn originates when we become the emissary of a message that has nothing to do with the Messenger. On the contrary, if we are saying something and someone likes it we will be rewarded, believing we did something good for this person. The Messenger was just a Messenger, who delivered a message, and has nothing to do with what resounds in the mind of the person that received it.

We also have people that has done some work on themselves; they don't get angry or happy with the Messenger, but they will be angry or happy with the message. They are not yet free from the circumstances, they are still identified with the message and still taking it personally; acting emotionally as a response to what was heard.

Finally, there are people who do a great job at discovering themselves; they separate the Messenger from the message. What they will take will be the part of the message that resounded within them. They will not react according to this, but take that resonance as an opportunity to self-observe and see what is affecting them from that message and how. With this opportunity they will be able to take the received messages as a map of their own being.

A mind that is not under control will easily take every message personally, and not just that, they will also create fantastic stories around the message, generating a snow ball effect, forging a big problem from that little excuse. This kind of activity will create a lot of emotional instability. It has a lot to do with the way that mental agitation works along with subconscious, ego, unstable mind and intellect.

«She told me goodbye with a voice tone that is different from the one she usually uses. Is she angry at me? Could it be that she doesn't love me anymore? (...) And last week, when we were having dinner with my friend Ernesto, she was very friendly. Could it be that they are both cheating on me? Are they having an affair (...) And last night, she asked me how I was doing at business. Could this mean that she wants to get a divorce or is she measuring how much she is going to take from me? (...) And also I wonder about my health. Could it be that she es planning to murder me along with Ernesto, take my

fortune and run away together?»

This example might sound funny, but this is the way that many minds work. Such out of control, that they will create a great story and suspicion from such a simple excuse as the change of other's voice tone. This is what makes mind out of control; it gets carried away and it creates a big trouble out of a small thing. Then, this mind that is out of control will act with its friend and partner according to this generated mental picture; There will be no more sweetness, but suspicion, and it will even be able to recreate the projection of what was imagined.

7. THE OPTIONS

Sometimes a look from the other, the interpretation of a look from the other, opinions, what people say and their vicissitudes, take place with the person's actions. Many people do things not because they want to, but to please others. They don't follow themselves, but others. They act according to what they think the other will think. They don't say what they want to say because they are afraid of how the other will take it. They don't do what they want to do because they are afraid of how the other will take it. How many times a day a person says what they want to say and do what they want to do? How many times a day a person says what they don't want to say and does what they don't want to do? Maybe it is about stop acting according to others, but according to oneself. And when we work according to oneself, it will be useful to follow what is known as the essential being and not fake personalities, that are built according to comparisons.

Acting for oneself saves the world, acting according to foreign interpretation confuses things. It is like losing the present because of fear to the future, instead of living what there is now to guarantee what can't be guaranteed. If we cultivate the in inside, we will give better things to the outside. There will always be an opinion that is going to find the negative side of things. There is no problem whit this happening; the problem would be listening to that and acting according to that; making decisions according to what others would think. Opinions are not the main problem, but believing in them. When we do it we are taking them; we identify with them, accept them, incorporate them, and deposit them into the subconscious, and the ego will identify the essential being with that opinion, it will define itself according to opinions and it will start acting according to them. That's how you build fake characters; personalities that are built up according to opinions, disguises that adequate to other's satisfaction. This fake personalities hide the essential being, one gets surrounded by them to present oneself towards the world, under the desire of being loved; believing that we are not going to be loved for what we are and that we need to satisfy others, even against ourselves, in order to receive love.

We don't need everything that comes to us. We don't need useless things inside our world. We don't have to take everything that comes just because it comes, and accept it. Many things that come to us are not meant for us. They could be the exteriorizations of someone else who has not worked on themselves. Not every critique, opinion or point of view has to do with us. If we accept and take every opinion we are given about ourselves, the game is over. The possibility for evolution won't exist, it will only be an accident after the other, following a sick current. There will always be opinions that are against us, no matter what we do. Society and its generality does what it doesn't want to do in order to get what it doesn't need. Following an uncontrolled gang won't be the best tool to discover our essential being.

«I don't know the key to success, but I know that the key to failure is trying to please everyone.» Woody Allen

There will always be opinions; for every existent possibility. We will find them in every decision we make; points of view that can be in favor and against it, There isn't an activity that can only generate only positive points of view. We can find a negative opinion in every event, in every circumstance, and also positive and neutral opinions and its infinite shades. There will always be diverse opinions. But if we take opinions and act according to them, it will cause us a lot of problems. People who behave by measuring themselves with the opinions of others, get into trouble.

Less opinion, more being. Less non-being, more being. Considering more what I feel, need and what every situation requires. It is not about taking everything that comes to us blindly, trying to please others without paying attention to what our being is telling us. Maybe it is all about taking what others want, say and do as signals to work with our being; observing if there is any inner reaction in front of that reflection, and maybe, depending on the situation, recognizing what is happening to us, how is it affecting us and why.

8. DIVERSITY

When we talk about god, the creator, the essence, the absolute, or whatever name you want to give him, within different religions, we can observe the same characteristics: omnipotent, omnipresent, in every space, in every place, in every time, infinite, absolute, perfect, eternal. This is the essence when it shows its visible face, when it manifests, it starts from a single spot and spreads into extension as a diversification. This could be the first thought that brought us here: the first thought about this divinity that starts expanding in different ways of manifestation. We are talking about something that seems to be a unity; it occupies the space, it can't be measured, and it includes everything within itself. But the world we live in is a dual world, and it comes in opposite pairs. Thanks to this duality, time is created. With the triad, then, space is created. When we come to this plane, manifested, we are ruled by different laws. For example, one of them is that everything come in pairs: day and night, man and woman, action and reaction. Maybe the birth of duality is due to the extension of the unity that wasn't yet part of the pairs game. Within the unity, we were all contained into the same space. Nevertheless, when the unity extended to its gestation –the two-, it started to enlarge and offer duality and time. Then, maybe it extended to space –the three- and gave birth to it. And It will continue from number to number, from attribute to attribute. When the unity extends itself to generate duality, diversity is generated. This extension of the unity allows the emergence of diversity, and it includes the tension and pressures generated by the extension and emergence. Within the unity we used to experience everything at once, containing the past, present and future into an eternal time; encompassing everything into one single form. However, when the unity extended, it offered us diversity, different ways, time, spaces, and then, possibilities. A natural tension is created by the emergence of the unity, by the emergence of diversity. Unity separates itself by extension, and it creates tension between two, and this is how diversity emerges. If we emerged from the apparition of the unity, when we are born, we extend from the unity to take part of diversity. This tension offers us differences, diversity, a universe of options and possibilities. In the same way it also generates a return to our source, as if it was a rubber band that extended from the same unity and generated pressure so it comes back. It is then, when an attraction and natural tension appears towards our diversity. This could be showing the loving and fearful nature that we have towards our source and others. We live in constant love and fear towards the divine and others, with a strength that impels us to join the other, to join God, and there is also a strength that impels us to fear others, to fear God.

Somehow, this creates tension between us. It is the natural difference. It is instinctive. Nature is afraid of what is different. The most primitive being will be comfortable with peers and it will feel awkward with who is different. A primitive being will need to form a group, a clan, with those who share something with them, because this way they will feel more contained. And they will point the different out as 'Bad'. The most primitive being will generate and identify with countries, soccer clubs, flags, cultures, languages; but others will still be bad!

A mind that is not controlled will take this separation and identify with it, it will take fear and identify strongly with it, it will take diversity and differences as fear, as an opposite rival and not as a complement. Maybe we are all part of the same unity and the natural fear that emerges from inside towards the difference is a condition that comes, but that is not necessary, it happens, but we can train ourselves to discover that everyone comes from this very root, with the manifested form that each one incarnated; we can love, learn and complement each other from this difference. We can take it as a tool to discover more about our purpose, our roots and our essence.

If at any time we realize this and learn from the differences, we will take them as an extension from the same root we come from. Maybe, in the future, every flag will disappear, we will become global citizens, our country will be planet earth... And maybe then, another conflict will start: rivalry with other planets and beings. Until someone says «Guys, don't fight, we all belong to the same galaxy». And from that moment on, we will all join into one galaxy and start conflicts with other galaxies. Until someone says «Guys, don't fight, we all belong to the same universe».

Maybe we will start learning from the difference instead of fighting it. An uncontrolled mind will try to change the other; a trained mind will change itself. A mind that gets trained can learn from differences, complement with opposites instead of rivaling with them, they will use words and behave carefully, checking what they say and which messages they tell the world. They will know that they can't change anyone and that the best they can do is with themselves; it is not about showing off, but about working with oneself; the best explanation is the example and it is not about forcing, but about proposing.

CHAPTER 6

SELF-EVALUATION

1. MEASURING OURSELVES
2. THE POWER OF WORDS
3. THE POWER OF THOUGHTS
4. SELF-REVIEW
5. HOW TO BUILD THE NON-BEING
6. DESIRE

1. MEASURING OURSELVES

Why do I do what I do?

People who train their minds will ask themselves this questions as they move forward; they will face each thought they have, each word they say and each thing they do. It is useful to check what our souls are wearing and each time we execute a form of its actions.

When we move forward in the training of our minds we will take care of our thoughts, words and actions. We will be aware of each one of them before proceeding, knowing that it is the first determinant of its becoming. We will check if what we think, say and do is useful for us and the world. We will take care of thoughts, words and actions with ruthless attention. We will check if it is about externalizing our opinion, points of view, answering or playing a deviant game, or if it is about giving something that can be useful for ourselves and others. We will be constantly wondering, Do I have something useful to say?, Why am I about to do this?, Does this offer anything to others? With ruthless attention we will be moving forward quietly, saying words when they are useful, offering actions when it is required, offering thoughts when there is an objective to define, address or organize.

On the other hand, whoever works in the training of the mind knows that their health depends on not being stuck, that we shouldn't be carrying things, and in case of doing so, we should express it healthy in order to take it out. When we express it healthy we won't give it to the other as a repressing thing, but find the way of creative expression that can heal. This way we will take anything that was stuck without affecting the other negatively, without stunning or exhausting, nor wasting vital energy.

2. THE POWER OF WORDS

The power of words is infinite; even if not seen, even if after a few moments they are not heard anymore, all the emitted words continue echoing in the universe. Every word we pronounce affect us, it affects the other and the world. Every word that is said work as an affirmation –positive, negative or neutral: according to the polarity in which it has been expressed-. Every word we pronounce work as a command that is sent to the universe.

When we define ourselves, we are sending this command to ourselves; the ego will identify with de definition and we will start acting according to it. Every definition we perform on ourselves is limiting. As we contain the infinite and the absolute potency in ourselves; when we define ourselves, we are restricting against the inner god that is breaking through the self. This is why it is also useful not to externalize everything that comes to us and not to act according to reactions, but paying attention to everything we are thinking, saying and doing (preferably before we do it).

«*...And be careful of what you do 'cause the lie becomes the truth.*» *Billie Jean. Michael Jackson*

Whoever says: «life is a fight», must be prepared for war, because life as a fight is the command that is being sent. Whoever says: «I want to die», must be very careful in how they move, because they are sending this command to the universe. Every affirmation we make becomes a sent command; and the universe will answer us according to what we are asking.

3. THE POWER OF THOUGHTS

We can get to almost any place through our thoughts. It is the underlying tool with which we have to become masters of our experience through this life.

It is useful to examine what we let in and what we let out, what we take from the world and what we give to it. It is about controlling the mind's nourishment. Everything we let in will act as an active influence over our minds; we will think according to what we eat with our senses.

Thoughts not only affect us, but also travel faster than light speed. A focused and trained mind will think about someone on the other side of the planet and will perfectly send that thought through. Furthermore, a very well trained mind can send a thought to another planet in another galaxy, and it will be delivered.

Telepathy can be practiced. There are many lines of thought working at the same time… and they can collide. If they come across, many things come to us, while we live, while we do every activity. At first, stimuli comes to us from our most close beings, from everyone that think or get excited about us; then those that interact with us during the day, even if it is casual; not only that, also from those that are sending advertising messages while we walk along the street; not only from that, but also from what is happening with the advertisement in other country, also what happens in another planet; hence, we get what happened and what will happen.

For some people that study the elixir of eternal life, the key to eternity is not to stop our waves. Matter is not more than waves. The most dense waves form dense matter, but they exist in a subtle field (thought, emotion, radial waves, etc.) Those who study how to reach eternal life, say that for this purpose, it is necessary that these waves don't stop. By working to continue this waves and not to stop them, it wouldn't be strange that a body could live 10,000 years.

4. SELF-REVIEW

Those who work on the training of their minds will know that the best you can give to others is the best you can give to yourself. Those who cultivate themselves work for the world. Those who know themselves irradiate their knowledge into the world.

Those who try to change the other, fight against the world. Those who work on training the mind will know that against any situation there is the possibility to accept it, change it, or getting away. They'll know that if they accept it, the whole of it without hesitation, will play with no other choice (at least until there is a new doubt to move forward). They will know that the only way to change a situation is changing themselves. They will know that to get away, it must be done without hesitation, closing with forgiveness, asking for forgiveness, forgiving themselves, being thankful, letting go and keeping moving, without leaving anything pending, closing healthily to give themselves the space to get inside de new.

Those who work on training the mind will know that sometimes it is useful to open all the doors and those that are not (the option that you choose) will close by themselves. That it is not necessary to fight, but to dare with flexibility. That faith with conscious actions is useful, while blind faith without actions has no results.

Those that work on training the mind will know that true peace exists between opposites. Many people who announce peace are generally alike: two people who share things, who have things in common, then, find themselves comfortably while talking about peace (or two nations that have traded agreements, or two clans that share something, among others.) Those who work on training the mind will know how to find themselves at peace with their opposite: there is where high peace sits, in learning the difference, in tolerance, in acceptance. Those that have move forward while training the mind wouldn't even find opposites.

5. HOW TO BUILD THE NON-BEING

The essential being that lives through each one of us is invisible. It can't be seen, not because it is hidden, but because it's been covered under many layers. We work as an artichoke, you can find its heart underneath all its leaves. The same way, behind all personalities, you can find fake selves covering the essential being.

The non-being are these disguises that are covering our essential being. The uncontrolled mind defines the essential being through fake selves, innocently believing that their being is their non-being. It defines the essential being through personalities, the names of those personalities and the characteristics that they get attributed. But the essential being is not the fake self. These personalities are built excuses to go through the world, disguises that we put on the essential being, believing that it will be useful to be loved, to achieve what we want, to make wishes come true or to cover necessities.

These fake personalities are built from the moment we are born. We start at a level of childish awareness, and we adapt to the world by imitating the examples we see. In case that the child wasn't born in an illuminated family, in an illuminated society, it starts taking odd examples. In that case, examples are given by people that are not being who they are, in which their essential being is not in the light and they don't live the life they deserve. We start oddly, constructing fake personalities based on imitating odd examples.

Then, the child moves forward to the development of their natural rights; during the cycle of the first seven years of life, children develop their natural rights of having, feeling, doing, loving and being loved, their right to see and know. Perhaps the child is in contact with a family, culture, religion, education, society and a world that doesn't encourage them to develop their natural rights and, on top of that, they are also repressed. If this happens, the deposit of restrictive ideas in the subconscious will be added to their fake personalities, that make the essential being not to express freely and not to wholly be. Then, as they grow up, maybe they will seek to love and be loved, and to achieve this, maybe they won't do what's right, maybe they don't follow the command from their essential being, but do what they think is convenient in order to receive love. Maybe they don't respect themselves and become unable to express freely. Also they might add authorizations and incorporate the opinion of others. When taking other points of view as our own, they will be deposited in the subconscious, and the ego will identify with them, and it will start acting according to what others say. It will act if the other authorizes it, it won't act so if the other doesn't authorize it, and it will move from accident after accident, like a sailboat that navigates on waters impulsed by opinions, points of view and odd beliefs. The weak ego and uncontrolled mind will join to, and will also take the opinions of others as their own and build fake personalities based on it. For example, the child will go to school, will interact with other children and teachers and suddenly will find that one day someone will tell them: « You are so Smart!». The children will believe and accept everything they are told, and maybe incorporate those words as commands and accommodate them into the subconscious. Maybe one day the child will be told: «You are terrible at sports!», and will take that «You are» as an excuse to define the essential being with the definition and manifest it; the disguise of being bad at sport will be on (maybe the child won't dare to get education on sports, move the body, or work on this area, because the command would be already deposited, identified, and solidified). This way, the child will be told many things, they might believe it or take them. They will be accommodated in the subconscious, the ego will identify with it, and it will go through the world managing through everything that is useless and it's been let in, because they would have believed it, accepted it and incorporated it. They will integrate commands such as «don't do this», «don't touch that», «close your eyes», «don't put that on your mouth», Everything that is told to children will become a command as they grow older. New archetypes will also be let in, as universal laws that will command fake truths, and incorporate them as their truths: teachers, doctors, lawyers, professionals at any discipline, bosses, partners, friends, every person will be taken as law and what they say will become part of their truth. They will make of voices, commands, and from these commands, laws. Then, the essential being will be far from living in plenitude, from doing what it wants, saying what is wanted to be said, feeling what is wanted to be felt, and living what is wanted to be lived. Now, the essential being, will be under layers and layers of fake selves; personalities built to adapt to a world that will do what they don't want to do, and get what they don't need. Now the essential being will be covered by layers of self-friend, self-son, self-daughter, self-husband, self- wife, self-father, self-mother, self-worker, self-teacher, self-citizen, self- student, among many others.

For a while one can believe we are comfortable under these disguises. However, this will be finite, time limited. At some point the disguises will start to feel awkward; the being will not feel comfortable with its fake personalities. It discovers that they are not doing what they want, but what they think they wants, or what others want or don't want, or what pleases others but not what pleases them. The being discovers that it is not telling what it wants, but it is talking according to certain protocol, that follows a programming or hypnosis state that doesn't represent it, that the language that it is using is awkward and doesn't allow it to say what it wants to say. It discovers that it is not living the life it wants, that it is carrying a life based on persecution and paranoia, that it spends time with those who doesn't love it, that it does what it doesn't want to do, that it lives where it doesn't want to, that it eats what doesn't nurtures it, that it lives a life that doesn't belong to it and doesn't develop its gifts, that it is far from looking for what is behind its desires, but it is more focused on covering the essential being with deviant commands: on being entertained with junk, on silencing it with drugs, on intoxicating with a useless life. It discovers that it is not giving to itself what it deserves, that it is not connected with its life, that it is not connected with the world, that it is not connected with others, that it lives in ridicule theaters taking the roles it was used to. Then, it realizes that it is failing on something, that the disguise doesn't fit anymore, that the life it is living is not the one its essential being calls to live.

Then, some drown on suffering and self-destruction, while others start looking for alternatives. Some look for options to get distracted; they cover and cover with layers, they cover a failure with another one, to keep going without facing their root. Others dear to go further, to start looking for alternatives, stop running and face their own darkness, to see what it is hiding with disguises, to see what is behind fake personalities, to know themselves more, to discover their essential being.

6. DESIRE

A mind on an uncontrolled state is chasing what will happen in the future, worrying about what is not here and losing the possibility to enjoy the present, sacrificing it for an uncertain future. An uncontrolled mind that doesn't know how to enjoy what it has, but chases what it doesn't have. An uncontrolled mind that doesn't channel desire, that can't even recognize it, but chase it and chase it restlessly.

The uncontrolled desire will always want more. To the one that holds ten you will give them ten and they will want a hundred; you will give them a hundred and then they will want a thousand; you will give them a thousand and then they will be desperate for ten thousand. Uncontrolled desire causes constant dissatisfaction; it always causes to want more, it never gets you satisfied, it doesn't let enjoying nor seeing what there is, it makes you chase what there isn't, it doesn't allow to work on desire but on the object of desire, it doesn't let us observe the power that moves us, that is within desire itself, but makes us hunt the object believing that there is an answer there; seeking outside what is in the inside. It is not about anything else, it is about what there is, to give it the best use possible and enjoy it. It is about channeling desire. If more arises, or less, it is about to channel those desires. It is about giving the best use possible to what there is. It is about observing what is moving us, the desire itself, that has the potency to wake us up in the morning and take us to execute actions.

What we need is different from what we desire. We need water, food, shelter, a bed, a roof. Our desires start from sexuality, our needs start from the body. Needs have to do with survival. Desire has to do with the purpose that brought us to the world; behind every superficial desire, behind all temptations, all ideals, there is the deep desire that brought us here and that motivates us to incarnate.

Desire doesn't stop in life, because it brought us to life. Channelled desire focuses us towards the effective search and the training on mental education. Desire in a uncontrolled mind agitates the mind and chases outside restlessly. This sort of desire generates a lot of mental agitation and mental dispersion.

It is not about desire, but about channeling desire and working from the engine of desire itself, in order to discover our own purpose, our gift, our deep desire within the depth of our unconscious. This kind of work gets done knowing that what potentiates us is not the object of desire, but desire itself.

CHAPTER 7

MENTAL GROUND

1. TEMPORARY HAPPINESS AND PERMANENT JOY

2. SUBTLE FIELDS

3. THOUGHTS AND EMOTIONS ARE REAL

4. NUTRITION OF THE MENTAL BODY

5. FROM BODY TO MIND

1. TEMPORARY HAPPINESS AND PERMANENT JOY

There are those who believe that happiness is outside and is the result of obtaining the object of desire. This type of happiness translates into constant persecution. Then, they will be bored with the toy and leave it, desire will return, happiness will vanish, unhappiness will return, and the pursuit of a new object of desire will be resumed.

The joy of being is different from the happiness of obtaining. The joy of being is something intrinsic that belongs to each one: it is about the enjoyment of being oneself, of wanting and being mobilized in the search, of enjoying each one of the steps along the way, of understanding each one of the experiences and live them in fullness, without despair; because the important thing of achievement is not in the achievement itself, but in the work done to achieve it (which will result in reaching us); because the important thing of the road is not the goal, but the search. Whoever manages to enter in themselves will discover a permanent joy that accompanies them; perhaps it is not as spectacular as the obtaining of a mansion or a Ferrari, the obtaining of the external object of the desire, but it is more lasting, because it accompanies us day and night, in each one of the steps, in each one of the results; whatever it is.

2. SUBTLE FIELDS

Think of jealousy, suspicions, and the quantity of real emotions that we can generate in imaginary situations. The fact does not have to be true for us to be able to feel it. If one constructs his feelings on the basis of falsehoods, we will found a life experience according to illusions; we will live in our fantasy, without ever touching reality. What could lead us to ask ourselves: what is real? Is there anything that could be more real than anything else?

There are emotions that happen, they are real, regardless of whether the fact has been false or not. Who works as an actor knows very well what I am saying. One thing is to pretend and another thing is to be. When a person pretends, perhaps they understand an idea but don't believe it, maybe they are not feeling it, then they will see the lie and they will be able to represent a feeling according to this, but they will be far from being and feeling. When a person feels the idea, it does not matter if it is a lie or not, because when they feel it, they will become and experience it as if it were a truth. A great actor is the one that feels what they are living, the one that is what they act out. A not so good actor may be who pretends, who understands what is being lived, but does not feel it.

This is how ideas work in our lives too. Ideas that are only assimilated intellectually can be understood, but will not be experienced. When ideas are taken as truths, they begin to be felt, experienced as truths, regardless of whether they are authentic or not.

Behind this lies the supposed reality in which we live. To be able to act we need to be able to experience, and to be able to experience we need to be able to feel. We do not know if it is true or not, if it exists or not, however for us everything that we live is real because we are feeling it, because the mind took it as a truth. Everything that happens is not necessarily true, but it is our truth at the moment it happens.

Many times what we feel has nothing to do with what is happening, with the truth or lie of the fact, but it is related to what we are taking of that and to the part that we make our own truth. What we feel responds to this small part that we access. So, there are lies that are sacred and truths that are useless. The important thing will be what resonates in us facing each circumstance.

3. THOUGHTS AND EMOTIONS ARE REAL

Although we do not see, we do not hear, we do not smell, we do not touch and, we can't feel the taste of thoughts and emotions, they exist. Both work in a subtle field that we can not distinguish them by the five classical organs of perception; however they are there, all the thoughts and emotions generated by us and by the other beings present on this planet, plus those that come from other planets, influencing and affecting us constantly. We do not see it, however in the most subtle field there is an energetic war, thoughts and emotions flying between bodies and bodies, fighting for who crosses who, absorbing vital energy one from another, sticking to the bodies of innocent children, on the walls of homes and on our bodies.

They are not seen, but yet exist. Scientists have not yet put a thought or emotion in a can and say that they got it there; however, they exist. The same way we don't see radio waves, internet waves, telephones calls' waves, they are around us, being both emitted and received, getting through us, affecting us. We don't tend to perceive them because we are limited in the way we manifest. We see the seven colors of the rainbow and its combinations, but we can't see more colors than these. We hear from certain frequencies to others, but we can't hear ultrasound, neither infrasound. There is a undulating frequency spectrum –sonorous, luminous and electromagnetic- which we have access to; we don't know what is happening further from this spectrum, ahead and behind, and there are levels that we can not perceive. We are limited. We come to this world with some things and without others. If we are aware of this, we will know that there are many levels of reality that are happening in a simultaneous way in which we are perceiving, that are happening on this instant around us, and we can't perceive them. However, they can affect and influence us (this would explain the world of ghost that live among us). Thoughts and emotions travel on this level; on fields so subtle that we can't see them, but they interact with us, and they are here, around us.

If we are able to understand this, and maybe comprehend it: what do we want to put on this world?, which thoughts and emotions do we want to send to our body and other beings' bodies? which thoughts and emotions do we want to fill our environments with?, which thoughts and emotions do we want to cover our home with?, which thoughts and emotions do we want to give our children? If we can remember that thoughts and emotions are real, we can measure which thoughts we throw and which emotions we are communicating. They are, even when we can't touch them or feel them, they are there, and they affect us.

And not only that; maybe thoughts and emotions resound as waves and keep existing after and before being perceived. Maybe everything we think and feel keep resounding in the universe and won't disappear from the subtle field. If this is so, it is not free to think or feel; it generates things that affect us, that affect others and maybe it will come to us. Everything we do, say and think goes to the world, and gets thrown to the universe, and then, somehow, it comes back.

If we exercise self-observation, we will find out that most of the thoughts and emotions we are experiencing are repetitive. We are wasting a lot of vital energy by not putting attention on ourselves and control our powers. Furthermore, we are sending chaotic commands to the universe and we are affecting the world that surrounds us without measuring how we do it. This happens because we are not observing ourselves.

If we pay attention, we will find out when we go to the streets that there is an energetic war; it is filled with energetic vampires that don't realize that they are sucking the vital energy to the one that is next to them (and filled of innocent donors of vital energy that is leaving them empty until becoming energetic corpses).

If we remember, we will start to use self observation more often to decide what we will do with thoughts and emotions that come: if we throw them to the world, if we feed them, or if we are indifferent toward them.

4. NUTRITION OF THE MENTAL BODY

Our physical body is built with dense matter that we take: the physical component of food. Our mental body is built with subtle matter that we take: the subtle body of food.

Let's think according to how and what we eat. And we will not only be thinking according to what is being introduced to our body orally, but also, we will think according to what is being introduced to our body visually, sonorously, physically, and olfactory. Our thoughts will work on the base of everything that gets inside of us. It is useful, then, to check what we are letting in and how we let it in, because according to this it will be the form of how we think, and according to the way in which we think it will be the way we live.

Food

Some food can generate excitation to the mind, other, tranquility, and other heaviness. Food like sugars and meet excite the mind, they give it passion and don't let it rest. Food like pasta and white flour are heavy, makes you lethargy and don't let the body act. Food like fresh vegetables and fruit give tranquility, calm and harmony.

Others

Positive and negative waves get to the mind through our eyes. When we dialog with someone that is negatively charged, and we stare at their right eye (which transmit us this vital energy), we would be absorbing part of their negative energy. The same way happens if both bodies are at short distance (close enough for the auric fields to contact) or if one of them closes their channels (chakras) and the other puts themselves in front of us. Such kind of internal contact is useful when both are charged with positive energy, then, there will be a positive dialog to give and receive. Being the case that one of them has negative vital energy, it is useful not to give it to others, but express it healthy and release it by using natural ways.

Sleep

Another of the great sources for mental nutrition is sleep. There are three types of states: vigil, light sleep and profound sleep. When we are vigil, the mind and body are switched on. When we are under light sleep the body is asleep and the mind is turned on. In profound sleep, the body and the mind are turned off. The mind really rests when we get into the state of profound sleep, when there is the state of light sleep, there is still mental activity (dreams).

The world we see is not the world that exists. The world we see is the world that our mind allows us to see. Everything we experience, through senses, is translated in the mind. If there wasn't a mind, we wouldn't be able to feel, neither experience this life we are living. What we see is the projection of our mind toward a certain object; we don't see the object, but the projection of ourselves –the subject- we put on the object. When we are in the state of light sleep, the object of observation has disappeared (we have our eyes closed), but the subject is still awake (the mind). Then, what the mind does is continuing to project; this time not on the base of the object of observation, but according to the memories and instincts anchored in the subconscious. Just when we are in the state of profound sleep, the object and the subject disappear, now there are no projections.

Breathing

The most subtle thing that feeds our minds is breathing. The body takes sun through the air. The better the being breathes, the better the mind will be and the easier it will be for it to focus, reach mental annihilation and not getting lost in mental agitation or dispersion.

Thoughts

Thoughts also feed the mind. Thinking too much is tiring, not thinking much gives it space, positive thoughts feed the mind positively, negative thoughts feed it negatively.

Administration of mental nutrition

The mind also feeds from what it takes from the environment, from companies, from others, and the type of movement we give to the body, the way we think and face each one of the circumstances and events that happen.

Many times, we don't pay attention to the food we are giving to the mind because it is not present; or it is acting or imagining something. If the mind is elsewhere when we do something, we will be absent. When being absent, we can't feel what happens to us and we become exposed towards the environment, willing to take anything without noticing.

If the mind is in the talk, in the critics, in judgments, in externalizing, in giving opinions, and in other ways of useless dialog, it will be spending vital energy, and if it does it while making a receptive activity, like eating, watching TV, it will be allowing things we don't need to get in. If we are present while we eat, while we move, while we dialog, while we act in the world, we will fill and know if what we are putting inside ourselves is useful or not.

5. FROM BODY TO MIND

Physical health is an outcome of mental health, and mental health is a possible outcome of physical health. It is useful to preserve and maintain physical health so our mental body doesn't take that much effort when functioning. Our physical and mental health depend on five activities we practice every day. We tend to perform them unconsciously, but we can change them in a voluntarily and consciously way, modifying health and the way that we live. These activities are the way we breathe, the way we eat, the way we move, the way we sleep and the way we think.[6]

---

[6] Lou Couture y Leandro Taub, Homemade Wisdom

CHAPTER 8

HEALING FROM THE MIND

1. MENTAL CAGES

2. OPENING OF MENTAL CAGES

3. PERVERSION OF MORALITY

4. WHAT'S GOOD AND WHAT'S NOT GOOD?

5. WHAT'S SUCCESS AND FAILURE

6. WITH LOVE AND FEAR

7. EXAGGERATED FEAR OR LACK OF LOVE?

8. STRENGTHENING ROOTS

9. FROM WORRY TO CONFIDENCE

10. THE NO IS ALWAYS THERE

11. THE PLANE FLIES THANKS TO THE HEADWIND

12. HARDSHIP STOPS BEING DIFFICULT WHEN IT STARTS BEING DONE

13. DOES SIZE MATTER?

14. A MATTER OF LUCK

15. TAKING THE TIME TO DO EACH THING

16. LET THE CAUSE OF THE SEARCH BE GREATER THAN THE CAUSE OF THE ESCAPE

17. WITHOUT ASKING FOR PERMISSION

18. BETWEEN DOING AND NOT DOING, ACTING

19. SUFFERING IS A CHOICE

20. GUILT AND REGRET KILL

21. HOLLY FORGIVENESS

22. EXPRESSING IN ORDER TO HEAL

23. DARK ILLUSIONS

24. EVERYTHING IS PERSONAL, AND NO THAT MUCH

25. DON'T WORRY, BE HAPPY

1. MENTAL CAGES

There are no greater limits than our possibilities. Many times we call «limits» what is only mental solidification, obstacles from a mind that is not trained and that works uncontrolled. These boundaries are built when the mind identifies with something and takes it as an absolute truth; in that moment an internal law is created, a sort of solidification that is transformed into spectacles, in their vision to see the world. From that instant it won't be able to see everything without judgment, now it will glimpse through that filter. That's how it will be unable to see everything that is happening, it will restrict itself and be a slave of its own identifications.

In other words, the uncontrolled mind identifies with its beliefs, opinions, points of view, ways, habits, costumes, and it defines itself according to this. The moment it defines itself, it identifies with this idea, it generates a solidification of this into the mind. From that moment the mind won't be able to see the world without judgment, but see through that idea —whether consciously or unconsciously anchored to our subconscious-. Then, the mind will restrict itself and see a filtered world, fragmented, denying itself to see the others. Summarizing: the mind will identify with an idea, it solidifies it, and becomes a slave of this and creates a boundary to see the world through that idea.

«I stay home on Saturdays, I don't like going out»; «I don't eat any vegetables that have been cooked with no other than wellspring water »; «Not this restaurant, I don't like it, I'd rather eat at others»; «This soccer team is the best, and not the others»; «I'm not competent»; «I can't»; «I'm anxious»; «I'm bipolar»; «It is a struggle»; «It is too hard».

This kind of mental cages not only restrict us, but also restricts our relationships, the capability to see others –It defines them in a way that won't allow to see them in any other way-; it restricts their work- we don't consider it capable of something, we define our qualities in a certain way and start to represent them, manifesting boundaries and living through them-; it restricts its prosperity- believing that we can't do it, that we are not worthy of wining, believing to be superior from others and it doesn't let us open our hearts and build relationships-.

The stronger the identification with these restrictive idea, the less will be the level of self observation, the more rigid will be the bars of the mental cell.

It is a great privilege to have a mental cage: we had to work a lot to build it, to identify with opinions, beliefs, points of view, among others. Then, it was necessary to solidify them into the mind, respect and accept them, taking them as part of the identity, confusing the essential being with characters, being a slave of them and moving through the world believing that the mask we were carrying was ours, living life through boundaries we have created, living life without being able to experience it as a whole because it is lived through a cage. This happens because when we follow the habits and costumes, without seeing other options and without opening ourselves to the possibility that other things could happen if we tried another option. Many people lay down without moving from their fake comfort, without pushing to get out of the limit, pretending to be comfortable when they are actually not. They are trapped in their mental cages, suffering without knowing why they suffer, limited, without putting any work on getting out, prisoners of their own buildings, blaming others and not taking care of their freedom. The power within everyone of us; each one is responsible of themselves and each one of us is equipped with everything we need to master our minds and work upon the knowledge of ourselves.

2. OPENING OF MENTAL CAGES

The first step toward getting out from conditioning is knowing that there is a conditioning, recognizing it. Once it has been recognized, it is possible to do the work of giving space to the mind; enough to be able to de-identify the ego from this identification and expand it.

In order to recognize the cages built where an habit or costume is, it only takes a day of self-observation: let's spend the whole day with a notebook and a pencil, and write down all the activities you've done. Write them in detail, how you felt, what you've done and how you did it. At the end of the day read this list and underline all the activities that you did that are regular in your lives. Do the same with all the repeated ways in which you behaved; do the same with all the emotions you felt. Everything must be pointed out, activities, ways and emotions, what's been repeated, they are habits and costumes that are solidified in the mind. It will be useful to do something different: if you tend to eat the same kind of food, try something different; if you tend to eat always the same way, try another way; if you tend to talk about the same subjects, try talking about other subjects; if you tend to get entertained in the same ways, try being entertained in other ways. It is about trying the different from the usual. This will give the mind flexibility and it will open it, offering it alternatives and amplifying its visual range.

In order to recognize cages built on the base of memories and instincts kept in the subconscious, it only takes paying attention to every reflex-thought or reflex-emotion; each time that a reflex-thought or reflex-emotion shows up, it is a sign that something has been kept in the subconscious and we are not recognizing it. In order to realize that, it is necessary to self-observe once again. When the reflex comes, instead of letting ourselves go with it, let's separate from our fake self and self-observe. Once we are under the magnifying glass of our analysis, we can start to wonder: what made me upset or what affected me from what just happened?, why?, why?, why? And so on. The game of the why (asking the reason of something and then wonder the reason of that answer, and then the reason of the next answer, and so on) allows us to investigate and recognize what is what we have kept in the subconscious that we don't want to recognize. Once it is recognized, it is useful to give ourselves space and the de-identify this memory from the ego. It is useful to transgress it, trying to do the things that we fear, in order to see that it is not a big deal to do it and deposit the authorization of getting out of it in our mind so we can for further the cage.

Every definition we make is limiting. Sometimes it is useful to define so we can channel an act. But it is also useful to unmake the definition once the act has been done. Defining oneself, defining others, defining relationships or defining the world is an unnecessary risk. Here comes the self-observation again; it is fundamental that we pay attention to ourselves and recognize each time when we are defining something. Once we recognize the definition we go back to the game of asking why: why am I defining this?

It is useful to give space and flexibility to the mind so it is not so rusty: recognizing our identifications and give ourselves the possibility to do the same thing in a different way.

There are no days alike, there are no nights alike, there are no beings alike, no worlds are alike, not even instants can be alike. In the manifestation everything moves forward, in a constant change and nothing repeats. This is a great sign to discover when we are caged in our minds; if there is a repetition, it means that something is hidden there. That's when the opportunities show to self-observe and recognize what is the repetition; investigate it to dominate it, give ourselves space and get out of it.

Getting out of habits, costumes, ways, opinions, commands and definitions, would lead to discovering yourself. You will see that your body, your sexuality, your heart and your mind are talking to you; that there are no repetitions and that every day tells you something different, something to work on and evolve with. It is about getting out of hypnotic states and programs with which we've moved forward, in order to give us the chance to change; because it is not something extraordinary, it is our divine right: changing and moving forward with life, to stop resisting it and allow us to live with life. If you dear to change, you will see how the world changes. If you dare to change, you will change the world.

«The definition of insanity is doing the same thing over and over and expecting different results.» Albert Einstein

3. PERVERSION OF MORALITY

The clans of education, culture, religion, politics, and fundamentally, family, tend to follow traditions blindly without ever considering the possibility of evaluating and measuring them; checking if they are useful, what and why are they there for. Many people behave without knowing this. «Why do I do what I do?», For what do I do what I do?» Traditions work through physical transmission, written transmission, oral transmission, and even psychological transmission of habits and costumes. Those who want to get out of the clan will have hard obstacles to do it –the famous black sheep- and investigating what there is further from that fake comfort about what is settled; what is further from the known world. It is useful to check our traditions and not respect them blindly, seeking why every thing happens and once it is known and recognized, take the decision to keep following it or not, if we do it this way or another. Whoever gets offended with people that leave the clan don't get upset because they did something wrong; who gets offended is disgusted because others are doing what they are forbidden to do. Every hassle that a person feels is the result of their reflection, they see in others something they don't allow to see from themselves, something that has been repressed or that is not being recognized; then the act of others brings them discomfort. The other did not necessarily do something good or bad, but just did what they did; and people that get offended by that receives a problem related to the lack of recognition of themselves. The more moral a person is, the more immoral they perceive the world that surround them. Whoever sees things as «bad» outside are the ones clinging in the inside, without recognizing themselves, without expanding, without investigating themselves, without getting out of traditions, costumes and habits, trapped in their prison of morality. How many relatives, friends, teachers, colleagues, students have gotten angry at you because you got out of what they think is their moral? What responsibility would you have for this? None. Getting angry is a problem for the one that got angry. And it is a problem that would be useful to check, because if there is an affectation it means there is something hidden there to recognize.

Perhaps morality is something that used to have an utility, and it was maintained with a cause and a motive; but as time passes by, it has been established and reached a moment where they keep sustaining habits based on that moral that had already expired, without knowing why or what is that for. What is terrible of this is not only the action through thoughts, words and physical acts that many people are sending unconsciously, but also, for them the world is defined according to this moral. They say that something is okay and other things are bad because they learned it so, but they didn't learn it according to their vital experience or their feelings; their learned it through intellectual transmission, empty of experience. They adopted crazy ideas that didn't belong to them and made them theirs, imitating completely unhinged examples and made them law, acted on resentment, guilt or regret and they projected it to the entire humanity.

Traditions tend to be the repetition in time of some activity that was once useful and it is not necessarily now. It has been forgotten why it was useful, and it kept being done and being interpreted arbitrarily. After transmitting them to their children, and them to their children, and them to their children, until it passed from generation to generation, it strengthened the rules and laws of the clan. Later, the seed was planted that to leave the clan is treason – Have you noticed the similarity between the word tradition and treason?-. The subconscious of the next generation came with the programming of respecting the clan and doing things well, and not doing what the clan says is acting wrongly. And if you don't respect what the clan says, if you betray the clan, there will be all kinds of punishments, even exile (an individual gets expelled from the clan).

There are several clans we belong to: family clan, friend clan, work clan, culture clan, soccer team clan, study clan, partner clan, children clan, among a long list. We form stereotypes of definitions, we execute them on ourselves and on others, we identify with them, we project them to the entire world and live through that filter. Then someone that doesn't belong to the clan arrives and says: «Comrades, we are all insane, this that you are doing doesn't work». And the punishment is enormous; the murder is contemplated because it is a treason to the clan, because of not following tradition, habits and costumes; because of not having respected their moral judgment.

In the world we live, there are countless religious confrontations based on having betrayed the clan, because of having defied it or done something that doesn't belong to its traditions.

It is useful to check what we do and what we don't, why we do it and why we don't do it, measure ourselves and estimate, check what is useful to us and what is not; choose freely no matter what tradition or moral commands. Maybe it is about recognizing the commandments that we have been imposed to, through which we have been accustomed to live for decades. Checking if these commandments have something to do with what the depths of our being asks us to do, and if our being asks us to do something else than what we are doing, follow. Maybe it is about checking the traditions we follow since we are little, our habits, costumes and check them very well, because they may disguise of us; they can be anchored in the subconscious, so identified with the ego, and so little recognized by their essential being, that we believe that what we are doing is our real selves. Maybe it is about observing the commandments of the clans that we took as universal laws and measure their distance from our center (if it is only a centimeter away, it doesn't belong to us); checking if we were programmed through reward and punishment, and we have deposited in our subconscious the crazy idea that if we do this in a certain way, we will receive the reward and if we do it in another way, we will receive the punishment. Maybe it is about checking the examples we copy since we were children, and getting out of the definitions of what the world is, about how people are, and allow us to see further from that and allow us to see ourselves.

When tradition, costumes and habits are repeated and respected blindly you are not seeing yourself, you don't know who you are, you don't even observe how you regularly behave; you are under profound degrees of hypnosis, without recognizing your true nature. The work we do with ourselves is about breaking the rules of the clan, not to fight with others, but to take the disguise off, which already feels very uncomfortable. And be careful when getting out of the clan; don't answer to threats, don't answer to attacks, don't answer to violence of those who are already in and see their actions as tradition. The level of identification with crazy ideas is so high that many people are capable of sacrificing their lives to defend a cause that doesn't belong to them, that they don't recognize, that doesn't belong to their essential being; but they are so attached to it that they wouldn't know how to do something else. It is useful to check for useless and harmful things that are being done and that are done to the world in order to keep following the rules of the clan, because of having them in our veins and arteries and not recognizing them, because of denying our own nature and essence.

There were times in history where killing wasn't a bad thing, but a need for survival. There were times in history where incest wasn't a bad thing, but a need for survival. There were times in history where eating meet wasn't a bad thing, but a need for survival. However, not because it was useful before it means that now it is. What is useful is not useful forever, the useless is not useless forever. Everything changes. Life keeps moving. Nothing remains (only the essence).

Once I was in a conference and asked: What does it mean to behave? Someone answered me that it was obeying. That answer made me shiver; he was talking about obeying the rules of the clans he belonged to, or believed he belonged to, he believed that behaving was to follow the commandments and misbehaving was to stop following them. I'd dear to change the definition of this «obeying»; maybe behaving was to obey, but not obeying the clan, but obeying ourselves.

4. WHAT'S GOOD AND WHAT'S NOT GOOD?

It would be useful to check what we call good and what we call bad, before we talk about good and bad.

Maybe, there is an association of the positive with the goodness, and the negative with the badness. If this is the case, we need both. How could we be here, living a manifested and dynamic life, if we only count with one of the polarities? We need the positive, negative and neutral polarities, as well as the essence to be able to be here. If this is the case, the moral connotation won't play any role.

On the other hand, we tend to associate what's bad with those who have a low level of awareness, with guilt, resentment or repentance inside, without being healed, without forgiving, without being free. Then, all that's being kept, instead of getting free of it in a useful way, it is being externalized with violence. There is a hurt child inside that wants to leave the suffering and externalizes it as it comes, unconsciously.

5. WHAT IS SUCCESS AND WHAT IS FAILURE?

They define failure as not being right, not achieving the objective, not being able to do what we have planned, getting an adverse result, not making it to the finish line or making it just after the other. They define success as doing as planned, achieving the objective, being right, getting a positive result or being the first to cross the finish line. If that is the case, we could only fail, and success would be disguised failure.

If we say that something happened as planned, we would be lying (lying to ourselves, then projecting that lie to others). In order to get something as planned, it is necessary to have such a powerful will that could move the will of the rest of the people on this planet. In case when we talk about someone who has that kind of will, that wouldn't be enough; we also need such a developed mental power with which we are able to influence the movement of stars, the dance of the spheres and the ascendant that this has in the self. In the case that someone had that kind of mental power, it wouldn't be enough yet; we also had to know the movement of the waves, their deviations and changes, counting with such developed intellect that would be able to calculate the following events with such perfect mathematical accuracy. Maybe this person has achieved something or many things, hence this achievement wasn't as planned, but the result of having worked, of having executed actions in full focus, with perseverance and without giving up. No one could plan or control what the rest of the humanity was going to do, say or think, neither how the stars were going to move. Maybe if we work, domain our powers, control our mind and doing useful actions. But this has nothing to do with our expectations or the achievement of them. The result, the achievement, it was what it was, and probably had nothing to do with what we could have imagined from the beginning.

There may not be success like achieving exactly what we planned; and there may also not be points of view about the same path (the fewer definitions we give it, the better it will be). Success, failure, they are relative. They don't have anything to do with the events we experience. There is higher intelligence working through us, and most of the things that happen are not being seen or controlled. But that minimum we control (what we think, say and do), if we do it mindfully, if we do it usefully, it will end up into great results. If we don't pay attention, if we don't self-observe, if we act impulsively, without noticing what we think, say or do, there will not be many things happening; and what happens will be associated, innocently, with «luck» and «bad luck». We would go bouncing from accident to accident, stumbling, without taking advantage of the powers we came equipped with into this manifestation.

6. WITH LOVE AND FEAR

We have several organs in our body. The negative organs are those that gestate, accumulate and incubate something; they are not transitory, but receive what comes and work with it for a while before the next stage. They are feminine organs, receptive, passive, negative, protective or fearful. The positive organs are those that transmit something; they are transitory, unstable, work as bridges or conducts, making the communication of our substances possible. They are masculine organs, penetrating, positive, active, transgressors or loving. Both form part of ourselves, and we need them both in order to incarnate into a body, manifest, live in the space and time, and experience the world. There are not good or bad types, but both are part of us. They are the needed polarities that dance through our center, our neutral state. All that, covered by the essence, it makes it possible for us to be here.

Fear helps us to protect, care, persevere, gestate, incubate. It is a receptive and pair attribute that stabilizes us and allows us to absorb and reveal knowledge, emotions, desires and necessities. Love helps us to transgress, to dare, to advance, to communicate and to transmit. It is the active and odd attribute that offers us the necessary instability to allow us to change, penetrate and execute actions, get out of our stability to go further, discover and expand, execute our ideas, open our heart and share, focus our wishes and make them come true, actuate in this world and cover our needs.

Our journey through this world is like the progress of numbers: from odd number to pair number, to odd number, to pair number, and so on (1,2,3,4,…). We appear (1); stabilize (2); explode by going out to the world to actuate (3); we balance on earth (4); we establish new ideals that make us jump further from the known place (5); we stabilize in pleasure, discovering what we like (6); we define objectives from what we want and execute them in the world (7); we achieve our work to stabilize in a fullness situation (8); we get out of the known world to pass our knowledge and go further to keep advancing (9); we close past cycles and open new ones (10). Our journey through the world oscillates as a pendulum between numbers; we pass from odd numbers to pair numbers, from loving acts to acts of fear, passing from actions to receptions, from giving to receiving, from doing to stabilizing.

There is not good or bad one, they are all positive as long as we keep moving. Stability helps us tho strengthen ourselves and plant; however, too much time stuck in stability, transforms strength into tyranny and the fruit will not sprout. Transgression helps us to advance and move the ground after the harvest; however, too much time moving in transgression, transforms the advance into an endless fight and the ground that moves after the harvest doesn't stop moving, doesn't leave space to new fruit, but keeps it in a continuous state of stress. It is not only about love and avoiding fear, but about getting the right measure for both things. Love is needed in order to transgress the established situation and advance to the next one. Fear is needed to protect and stabilize, to seat down and absorb what's been experienced, learn from it and preparing to the next step. One without the other becomes sterile. Without fear, love becomes pure transgression without ever reaching port. Without love, fear would be pure seating, it would be kept in a locked room, put inside a box, without discovering what's outside, without daring to see the world that's beyond. In a house where there is more love than there is fear, children transgress inside. In a house where there is more fear than love, children transgress outside; they will be fearful in the inside.

7. EXAGGERATED FEAR OR LACK OF LOVE?

We stand in a point of history where fear is attacked as if it was the world's enemy and love flags are being held as if it were savior. If someone doesn't allow themselves to do things, they are being repressed, if they are told to kill by fear, that fear is trapping them, and they can't get out of the confinement because of it. Playing the game of words: Could it be that fear is not the enemy, and those who don't allow themselves to do what they want do it because of a lack of love? If fear helps us to protect and love helps us to transgress, people who are confined in their stability maybe have an exaggerated fear installed in their subconscious, as it could also be that they are lacking love and that doesn't allow them to gain the courage needed to transgress. Both of them are useless and necessary, both are interdependent and work by interacting with each other.

8. STRENGTHENING ROOTS

If what stops us is an exaggerated fear, and lack of dare to immerse to the adventure of life, it is useful to check why this is happening and stop propagandizing against one of our polarities. A tree with weak roots falls beneath a great storm; a tree with big strong roots remains standing after it. What is the difference between both trees? Their roots.

When there is a good rooting, we count with a solid and strong base. Fear won't be a roof, but soil, it won't be what restrict us but what potentiate us. Love won't be something that's unreachable but something that's possible, we won't be talking about cowardice, but about bravery. Good rooting offers the confidence in the natural process, a stable ground to actuate upon. When there is certainty about the ground, bravery gets cultivated. The presence of earth in all its forms strengthen the rooting; it offers the baseline element that holds us. More roots give more safety, a solid base, a pillar, common sense, confidence in the natural process and strength. Less roots strengthen fear, nervousness, preoccupation and weakness. Confidence in the natural process offers understanding of the life's cycles, knowing that everything that is born dies, understanding that everything is changing, knowing regularity and discipline, and recognizing that emotions aren't ours, but they work as waves that are passing: that they have something to do with a being that is standing on a planet that is spinning around a star along with other planets, and that they are all spinning along with other systems around a galaxy, and that the galaxy is spinning along with other galaxies around a universe; and that all that affects us. In order to strengthen the rooting, it is useful to include more nature into our day, putting bear hands and feet on the ground, reconcile with the body, taking care of plants, animals, working on our background, working on the family tree, working on the Muladhara (Root) and Svadhisthana (sexual) chakras, balancing statements, balancing relationships, adding more physical activities and clarifying goods.

9. FROM WORRY TO CONFIDENCE

When the mind is in its most primitive state, it will be working within the mental agitation ways of acting and it will pass to mental dispersion whenever it has a hint of an objective. This kind of mind will be repeatedly jumping in space-time during the day; imagining things in the past or future, projecting, speculating, remembering, missing, among many others. When it is restless and needs the resolution of everything, it won't be patient, it will fall into despair of what's uncertain and will seek to create imaginary results to every future hesitation, with the purpose of not letting any space open. It will be preoccupied about everything that's coming. It will doubt if what we are doing is right, and worry about the next outcome; it will be worried about our loved ones, their work, their development, about itself, about the world, about a comet falling to the earth, and about the end of the world; it will be worried about every possible idea that installs in its mind and has the possibility to create a great snowball around that excuse.

Preoccupation is harmful to ourselves and others, including the world. When there is a worried mind, an unstable emotion gets installed into the environment and becomes able to create stress into everyones' present. As thoughts and emotions are waves that travel faster than light and travel long distance, each time that the mind worries, it is affecting the body that it runs, the beings around it and the whole world.

Additionally, preoccupation drains our vital energy, it wastes vitality when it generates mental dialog, it generates tremors in the emotional body, physical stress, and even possible health affections.

We are working here (in the present), taking care only of the thing we can take care of, about what is on the table, what we have at our disposal. Worrying means to focus on what we don't have on the table, instead of focusing on what there is. Worrying is about taking care of what isn't here, of what will come and has not yet arrived, focusing on solving something that doesn't require a solution today. This way difficulties appear and a problem about something that wasn't a problem, becomes one. It doesn't only affect the present, but also the future, changing its course. It often happens that the future its not given as expected. However, worries provoke its manifestation: attracting what it fears most, people that worry are capable to conceive the problem they anticipated.

Furthermore, unstable emotions that are put in the environment do affect; they will be throwing waves of instability that will alter you, your family, friends and the world.

A trained mind will know that the future is uncertain, that the unknown is the law in which it moves forward and that it is okay that it happens that way. It doesn't worry about what it can't control, but takes care of what is on its reach. It gives the best of itself on each one of the instants to construct, step by step, trusting in the future. It acts, trusts, and let go of what can't control to the unknown, with trust.

When we worry, we are trying to control something that we can't get busy with, because it belongs to the future. When we get busy with something, we are dedicating to what's in the present, on our reach.

Installing trust as a present tool and as a future tool is something useful to put along the work that is being done. Giving the best on each one of the instants is enough to do whatever we propose. The sun rises every day, it doesn't fail on its duty; nature lives through a natural process, and it does it really well. Instead of working to try to control the sun waves, or the frequency and intensity of the rain, things that are out of our control, we can trust that they will do their job for themselves. What we can control is little, and what we can control we do it the best way possible, without worrying about what is beyond our reach, and having an efficient use of time, giving the best of ourselves at every moment. This way, stone by stone, we will be building a castle.

If we are only thinking about the castle, we will fall into despair; we will see the immense construction, and we won't know how to build something like that, it will worry us and we will end up giving up without even trying, or trying and giving up at the first failure. We don't know how to do it, and we stand on nothing, or we try it, fail, and quit. We are eager to have the complete result, anxious, looking at the future, and not living the present, what there is, then we will fall in despair, see it too hard, impossible, we quit and go to do something else. It is not about the achievement, but about the work done in order to do it.

It is not about worrying, but about getting busy and move forward. The best we can do for the future sits right now, the best we can do for the past sits right now, the best we can do for us sits right now, and it is here. If it is not here, it is nowhere. It is about trust, about defining an objective, working with the mind, organizing it, guide it towards its direction and advance from present to present, from instant to instant, doing the best as possible each moment, and focusing on them, maximizing our giving in any circumstance. If we are making progress, it is already a big step.

10. THE NO IS ALWAYS THERE

When I was young, I was embarrassed to talk to women. I loved them, I wanted to ask them out, but I wouldn't dare. One day, my father told me something that changed everything: «The no is always there».

Behind that phrase there was something really big to be discovered; the no is always there. When we don't act, it is like it was a no, we keep on the stable state, without any change or news. When it is done, the no can transform into a yes; and if it doesn't happen, it comes back to the old no, but this time with one difference: we where given the possibility to learn something (and we talk about experiential learning, the one that comes as a result of experience and not theory).

Later, I took that 'no' beyond asking a woman out; I started to apply it on everything that I doubted and every situation in which I wanted to dare; it helped me to adventure; whatever I did, I knew that the 'no' was already present. And sometimes I came across some positive outcomes.

Then, I found that other 'no's' would show up; the 'no' from family, from friends, from society, from culture, from religion, even the 'no; for strangers. I discovered that the support from others is a remarkable thing, and that it is okay that it is that way.

The clan advances together toward a same direction, without wondering why they do it, without measuring what are they doing; they feel like they belong and that is enough to keep going without being aware of what they do, and why they do what they do. Suddenly, someone starts to wonder about these things; naturally, they will find that they are not running with the clan anymore, now they have stopped or are walking against the current. The result of this advance against the current will be resistance against the current. The 'no' of all that surround them. Some would use it to fight, some other will defeat the possibility of fight and will use it to potentiate themselves.

11. THE PLANE FLIES THANKS TO THE HEADWIND

Maybe, it is that very thing that makes us soar; it is not going against others, but letting go and advancing with the current and the inner current.

If we don't dare to get out of the command and start to set goals, defining a direction, even if we don't know how we would do it, it is possible to achieve something. As a consequence, it is not about worrying, but about getting busy; about get going, step by step, taking care of each one of the steps and making the best of it. That is how we can advance, how we can get somewhere. And then, we will discover what we have done. Maybe this is what it takes to search and achieve, and we will make it until the mystery receives us, guided by our steps. Then we will discover where we have gotten. Maybe this is the work that's needed to seek and achieve, and we will get to wherever the mystery welcomes us, guided by our steps.

12. HARDSHIP STOPS BEING DIFFICULT WHEN IT STARTS BEING DONE

We don't know how, we don't know it, we have never done it, it looks difficult. Would that be a good excuse not to dare? «I can't», I keep hearing during the day... why can't you? Why don't you allow yourself to do it? Why does someone tell you no? Why not trying? Why didn't you find the way? Maybe the «I can't» is the only barrier before acting.

Everything that's possible started as impossible. What is difficult stops being difficult when it gets done. Once it is done it stops being difficult, now it is easy. Once it gets done it stops being impossible, now it is possible.

If you see, most of the activities that are easy to you now, if you do a regression, you will find out that they once seemed difficult or impossible before becoming a habit: writing, talking, walking, riding a bike, maths. You had to dear, to put your intention and work toward that. The study didn't grant you anything, it was needed to put the body into motion and take everything to practice; daring to access to craziness and jump into action. Because intellectual knowledge is not enough to achieve something, it is necessary to take the idea down to the heart; experience it in order to feel and apprehend it. Before doing something that seemed complicated, once they did it, not so much. Constructing a rocket to travel the moon sounds pretty complicated; however, if you study and work on it, you start making it, step by step, you are capable to achieve it. Once you have done it you can look back and you will see the whole journey, it wasn't as hard as it seemed; and if it was impossible, you made it possible.

Difficult things don't actually exist; it is a definition, made out of stubbornness, laziness, identifications that create restrictions and a certain crazy futurism. What is difficult is used as an excuse, words used to justify the will of not doing. If you dear to do, once you start to work, you will see that what you have done until now wasn't as difficult as it seemed. Then, it is necessary to bring some options, to frequently access the unstable mind, to offer ourselves choices and different doors, or to break a wall, or to make a hole and building a window. Whatever it takes to access to more options and have no excuses to keep going.

If you define an objective, if you are deciding directions and organizing the present elements on each one of the instants, advancing and studying, you will see that everything is possible. Besides, the mind will entertain with something useful. It will be achieving, with patience; the expectations will be lowering, the miracle will be emerging.

13. DOES SIZE MATTER?

No matter if it is a big goal or a small one; if you propose an objective and keep your sight there, you might fall in despair, the mind will start to actuate wildly, negative emotions will be instated and finally, you will abandon the search. If you propose objectives and after you define them, lower your sight to the present, in order to mandate the mind to organize and decide directions, you might make it step by step, the path to achieve your goals.

Our journey works through fractals; a great objective includes small objectives; and each one of the small objectives include smaller objectives. The objective of writing a useful book holds within smaller objectives. The objective of writing a useful book holds within the objective of writing useful chapters, useful paragraphs, useful sentences, and so on. It is then that, to achieve any objective, no matter its size, it is necessary to focus on the present and get the mind busy in achieving each one of the small and insignificant purposes; each one of the stones of the castle, capable to build our own sacred temple.

14. A MATTER OF LUCK

The uncontrolled mind will define luck as a divine chance; some have it, others don't; in some circumstances we are lucky, in other we are not. Cheap superstition will define the situation according to the divine chance, according to good and back luck. Maybe it might not be as it looks. Maybe luck doesn't exist as a divine chance, but it might be the result of a construction and a dialog. Maybe luck is the encounter of preparation, chance and our dialog with silence; let's see the opportunity when we have our eyes wide open. It is very little what we can control; but if we focus on that little we control, things will change substantially. With that little we control, we can build our luck and stop waiting that something happens by chance or by matters of speculative superstitions, things will turn out as we seek them. With attention focused toward ourselves we can abandon the «Today happened this way, yesterday happened this way, so tomorrow will happen this way », «I got sick...How unlucky I am!», «I got a raise... how lucky I am!», and other forms of accidents that we don't observe. Maybe nothing happens by chance and everything is a network of causalities, and what happens to us is the result of what we think, say and do, plus our dialog with the mystery.

When we prepare ourselves, work toward ourselves and educate the mind, focus will be on taking the chances that appear and activating them. Focusing on what we think, say and do, maybe we will discover the network of synchrony and causalities that makes causality and luck fade away. We would be playing the game instead of suffering it.

15. TAKING THE TIME TO DO EACH THING

If we don't dare to start, and go from beginning to beginning, and do every step as best as possible, it would be useful to check the time we are taking to do each thing. If we take a distance from the mind, and we are not only training it, but also taking control of it, it would be useful to give it time enough to complete each thing we do. Not letting ourselves be carried away by mental dispersion, but doing each thing when it is desired, with full concentration and attention as it is possible, taking the time that it requires.

The uncontrolled mind will be stunned; it will see what it wants to do and try to do it at the same time. As a result, it will fall into despair and enter a phase of chaos, it will see many activities and not organize itself, it will be afraid and end up not acting or acting carelessly. Then, the person will end emotionally unstable, with a bad administration of the vital energy, bent, stressed out, without knowing how to face what they want to do.

It is not about the quantity of the things we do, but how we do them. If we focus on each detail while we act, if we take the time to do each thing, it won't matter the number of activities to do, everything will be possible, a thing at a time. It is about focusing on what we are doing, and once it is done, topping the inertia to pass to the next activity in full presence, giving the best of ourselves once again, putting full attention and giving it the time it requires.

The idea is to take the time to do each thing. It helps us to be present and not skipping the details.

16. LET THE CAUSE OF THE SEARCH BE GREATER THAN THE CAUSE OF THE ESCAPE

It is useful to check where our decisions come from and why we make them. Some decisions are moved by a search, because they go toward a direction, while others are moved by evasion, because we are running from something. Some other times, decisions are composed by both search and escape.

Whatever it is the influence of the decision, it is useful to check if the motive of the search is the greatest one; that we are advancing toward an objective and not advancing to escape. Because if it is a escape, the shadow will always follow. If there isn't something that was resolved in the past, the same obstacle will continue to show in the future; until getting resolved, it will keep repeating over and over again. That's the reason why there are too many people that change everything (external) and they don't really change a thing (internal). They live running, changing everything, and not modifying things because the focus of their lack of recognition keeps accompanying them.

If we make decisions moved by a search, our path will flow naturally (visualize a person moving ahead, looking forward). On the other hand, if we make decisions motivated by a wish of escape, you will move forward but looking backwards. If you do this, the result will be obvious: you will collide with everything that comes forward because you won't see it coming, you won't be paying attention to what's happening now and then, because you will be having your sight anchored in what you are leaving, what you are running away from.

If there is a conflict, it is useful to face it and solve it, not escaping from it. If you can't face it, take some time off, give space to the mind, de-identify with the affection, and when you find the sacred difference about it, go back to recognizing it in order to get a healthy closure; by forgiving others, forgiving ourselves, thanking, closing, and keep moving.

17. WITHOUT ASKING FOR PERMISSION

Don't ask for permission. You don't need the approval neither other's permission to be. Don't ask for permission. That is what children do when they are still under some level of awareness that they need to be told what to do or what not to do. In spite of this, there are some adults who remain under this level of awareness, then, they look for a partner or boss to tell them what to do. They don't need it anymore. Be responsible of yourself, of what you think, feel, desire and need. You are equipped with all the tools you need to have a full life. You don't need anyone's approval, neither their acceptance to be who you are. Dare to be without asking for permission.

18. BETWEEN DOING AND NOT DOING: ACTING

Let's go back to the beginning of this section; the 'no' is always there. Being aware of that impulses us to the closure of the chapter: between doing and not doing, acting. If we don't act because of fear to suffering, we will suffer because of the lack of action.

If a doubt has been open, if we have accessed to the unstable mind, if we have open the possibilities, the only thing left is to dare to move forward, to make decisions from the intellect, so we can go to our next state. If we don't dare to take action, we will remain doubtful and in full instability, or we will be moving backwards, depositing ourselves in state that could have been comfortable, but now we are closer to a fake wellbeing; to a hidden suffering. If they doubt is already open, daring to move forward can generate learning and evolution, no matter the result of the progress.

19. SUFFERING IS A CHOICE

Pain passes with time. Suffering is optional and it lasts as long as we keep it to ourselves. It can pass without being felt, it can stop, and be held for the periods in which we hold it mentally.

Suffering is a choice of a mind that is in an uncontrolled state, that takes something and repeatedly digs into it, creating a great problem toward an excuse. This uncontrolled mind is capable of taking this excuse, projecting suffering and working so hard on what's around that it access to the whole humanity's suffering. And not only that, but it is also capable of carrying it for life. It uses the power of concentration to pump suffering up, instead of taking useful actions, advancing toward defined objectives or fulfilling its wishes. It focuses on self-created dissatisfaction and fabricate a great story toward it.

Suffering is a master, one of the fiercest. It is the one that hunts us until we deal with what we have to resolve. It is a sign that puts itself in front and inside of us, shouting, asking for attention.

If there is suffering it means that there is something. And not something outside, but inside. Saying that we suffer because of something that is in the outside is an excuse, is externalizing responsibility to keep what we don't want to recognize under the shades. And as long as it is not recognized, there won't be a possible solution, it will become something that we won't recognize, and that will dominate us day and night, without seeing its face.

It torments us without knowing what it is. We can spend our whole lives without learning a single thing. We can spend our whole life without recognizing what is hidden behind our suffering, without understanding, desperate, without doing any internal work.

If there is any suffering, it is useful to turn it around, to observe the shadow and recognize what is inside of us and that is asking for help, to recognize what is that suffering; the reason why we are suffering and what it hides. Once it is recognized, it is possible to give us space, to take a distance and de-identify from the ego. In order to do this, it is necessary to submit to research; to look into ourselves and being the object of study of our own laboratory.

If you find it difficult to take a distance and suffering is very present, it is useful to pass to the active cycle: physical and mental activities that take us away from the passive cycle (in which the suffering grows without stopping), to be entertained by healthy activities, that give us enough space, so we see suffering from another perspective. Then, it will be possible to give space to the mind and de-identify with the ego, get pulled of suffering and seeing it as something small and insignificant.

Pain is another thing; pain is something physical and suffering is something emotional, that comes as a result of something mental. Physical pain passes; if you face and recognize it, it will last what it is meant to last and then it'll pass. It always passes away. It is inevitable when it happens. But if you don't identify with it, you recognize and see it, you will notice how it lasts for a while and then passes.

Suffering can be avoided. It will last as much as you want it to last. If you recognize it constantly, if you self-observe, you will master your mind and control your actions in the world, it is possible not to enter that suffering. In case it happens, if you keep on self-observation and training your mind, you'll be able to do this work quickly and not getting into the game, not digging, not making grow a suffering, not maintaining it, recognize it, recognize de signal, learn, be grateful, bless it, and get rid of it.

20. GUILT AND REGRET KILL

The «if» doesn't exist. The path you've taken was the only one that was possible. There is no turn back. Focus your attention on each present moment, because it is all you have. The more you give to the present, the more you will give to yourself. The more you put aside present, the more you will put aside from yourself. Once you've made a choice, don't look back, focus on giving the best of you in your path. Until a new doubt opens, until new possibilities open; then go back and look up, and choose bravely which will be your next decision; make it and go back to focus on your path, on each one of the steps, on giving the best of you in every moment. There is no turn back, there is no ctrl+z in life, there is no space for guilt, neither regret, there is no space to carry useless backpacks, there is no space for boycotting, neither killing us with useless things. Give yourself the best of you and give the world the best of you.

«Guilt doesn't help. The more time the being remains in the guilt's black hole, the more difficult it will be to get out, and if it remains for a long period there, it dies. Guilt has been transmitted from generation to generation over thousands of years. Knowing your source and functioning is fundamental in order not to fall into it. It absorbs vital energy and doesn't bring any news. When the being is immersed in the feeling of guilt, it doesn't work dynamically, it behaves like a zombie, incapable to relate in a nurture way and its presence will become unbearable to the optimistic environment. Morality that was

conventionally built to sustain guilt as a value or virtue is not useful for the being. Morality, that without experiencing, defines what's "good" and "bad" , derives us into useless guilt. Conscious morality is built through the experience of the being.»[7]

We live in a world in which guilt, regret and resentment is killing more people than wars. These serial murderers create diseases and kill on daily basis. They are not reproductive. They don't add anything. They don't vitalize.

Guilt and regret have been tools that have been very well used by those who wanted to domain masses through the years. When it is wanted that the oppressed concedes help, and they find themselves immerse into small problems and not seeing further from the cage in which they are put into, guilt and regrets are introduced. It has happened this way for thousands of years and it continues to happen. There is a huge amount of people that received an education based in guilt and regret, they carry this kind of affections throughout life and they transform into their big excuses not to allow themselves to be who they are, no to live their lives to the full, not to give themselves what they deserve, not to answer to their dignity of being alive and acting according to it.

If there is any guilt or regret, it is fundamental to free ourselves from it. Express it until nothing remains; not to others, not unhealthily, but in some creative or reproductive way. The best of guilt is not having it. There is nothing useful about carrying guilt and regret; the only thing they do is taking our attention away from the present and from what is happening, stun us mentally, install unstable emotions, take vital energy away, create diseases, and finally, kill us.

If there is any guilt or regret, it is necessary to ask for forgiveness and forgive ourselves, doing the necessary rituals to achieve that the being takes this new true as an inner law; to forgive the character and ask for forgiveness. If we do this, we will free ourselves from guilt. If we then achieve to keep moving, giving the best of us, we won't give space to the emergence of new guilt and regrets: because we know that we were doing the best possible, because we were giving the best there was in ourselves on each mo-

---

[7] Leandro Taub, Holy Devil

ment. And if some new event threatens to create in us guilt and regret, we shouldn't authorize that thought. If we don't authorize that thought, there won't be a possible emotion of guilt or regret. And if someone is trying to put responsibility on us about something, blame us, we shouldn't get into that perverse game, it won't be useful to take that guilt or accept that negative energy. And if that happens, we shouldn't let ourselves get carried away by the voices, and we create some guilt, it will be necessary to do the ritual and ask for forgiveness, and forgive ourselves, accepting the ritual and taking it, to heal that wound and keep moving.

The same happens with resentment, inversely. Resentment, on the other hand, creates guilt and it makes us externalize it; we are blaming others for our own suffering. This will be harmful for others and for us (in case others play the perverse game and take the guilt we are throwing at them). If there is resentment, it is necessary to do the ritual of forgiveness; allowing the being to take forgiveness as truth and law; forgiving and thanking; recognizing and taking the signal that is present in order to learn, forgive and keep on without looking backwards. And if a threaten of resentment appears, and we can self-observe before we get into that perverse game, it will be useful to check what is that we are externalizing, what was that, that hurt us, why has it hurt us. Searching inside to discover that others are not responsible, and they couldn't have been it, it is possible that everything is a network of causality and nothing happens by chance: searching to discover the sign and learning, searching to forgive and not carrying any weight.

If we hurt someone somehow, wither by thoughts, words or action, it would be useful to ask for forgiveness and forgive ourselves. Closing the wound and be free. Not carrying with useless things anymore and be loose through life. Honoring the emotions and making them sacred; blessing each one of the steps because each step has its reason of being. Closure cycles and not go into a vicious circles. Pulling off the psychological splinters that kill us. Closing what's passed and allowing entrance to new experiences, new relationships and ways. It was what it was. It is what it is. It will be what it will be. The past can't be changed. What we can do is heal it and keep moving; not carrying what's useless and living; putting sublime ideas in the mind and setting useful objectives. Being present with everything that give us life, and giving it the best of us.

In case there is guilt, regret or resentment, the ritual will be to ask for forgiveness, forgiving the other and ourselves, thanking, closing, letting go and keep moving. Practically or metaphorically, doing the practice and the ritual so the essential being takes it as truth, as a universal law, so it heals its wounds and not carrying with useless things. Asking for forgiveness and forgiving ourselves to heal guilt and regrets; forgiving to heal resentment; closing to give and end to that guilt, regret and closed resentment; thanking in order to bless the experience; letting go, so we don't carry with what we have closed and introducing into the divine; keep going, so we don't entertain with the past, forgetting anecdotes, setting useful objectives, choosing directions, organizing and keep on living.

21. HOLLY FORGIVENESS

The practice of forgiveness, in all its forms, releases us from guilt, regret, resentment and everything that could be dragged from the past. That is the key to open the handcuffs that ties us to the mental chains. That is the great master of the spirit of your journey through the world.

What has happened can't be changed, but the past can. We can't change what happened, but we can change how we see what happened. And if we change the way we see what happened, that changes what happened in our mind.

Most of the things we remember didn't happen as we remember them. We remember only the part in which the mind held the part of the experience that was deposited as a memory into the subconscious, in which the ego finds identification. If the memory is installed, we can change or erase it. Everything that got in can go out, everything that doesn't belong to us can be changed. Every memory of the past can be altered. And when we do this, it changes our perception of what we lived; influenced by our whole present and altering the becoming of things. Changing the memory of the past, we can change our future. We don't have the possibility to go back and change what has happened, but we do have the possibility to change the way in which the mind perceives what happened. And when we do it, everything is changed.

Forgiveness in all its ways is the tool that will de-identify us from the memories in which the ego finds rigidly identified with. Once we let go of those memories, once we stop carrying any more guilt, regret, resentment or its alternatives, we can reinterpret history, change the way we see it.

In case we proceed to honor the emotions, bless the experiences and sublimate them, we will boost the mind to get into the sacred forgiveness, taking off the stones of the past and move lightly, with no tormenting memories, neither chains from the past. It is freedom at its splendor; full acceptance, and sacred forgetfulness.

22. EXPRESSING IN ORDER TO HEAL

Express heals. What we hold is toxic and needs to go, which hinders the natural flow of our substances, which obstructs the circulation of the mind, emotions, sexuality or body. The water that does not flow stagnates. And where there is standing water, where there is poisoning, the disease can emerge. Express heals. When we express reproductively we are taking out what we were holding; collaborating with our circulation, and therefore contributing to the preservation of our health.

Expressing toward nature, expressing creatively, expressing through work, expressing through writing, expressing through painting, expressing through singing, expressing through sports, expressing through exercise. Every expression that unloads us, helps us to let go of what we were holding onto. That's why athletes are healthy; not only because of the physical work they do, but because when they play sports, they are working on a mental, emotional and sexual level: they are unloading themselves through physical movement.

Stress comes as result of retention; instead of fighting or fleeing when there is a threat, instead of expressing when something happens and we prepare ourselves to express, we are retaining that inner movement. We don't fight nor flee, we retain every inner movement (psychological, emotional, sexual, and physical); then, we get stressed out. We retain something inside that we are not letting go. Expressing helps us to get rid of stress.

When we add poor rooting to stress, when we install restrictive ideas, or when we are having a bad administration of our vital energy, we go from stress to depression. When we don't have a solid base, and we don't trust the natural process -not even understand it-, there is no strength only intellect, there is not comprehension of events, there is no feeling, there is no experience in flesh; a soft wind knocks down a tree; stress with poor rooting conducts to depression. And in that case, on the first place, it will be necessary to move to the active cycle, getting out of the passive cycle, doing physical activities. Once you go into the active mental plane, we will be able to strengthen the rooting; giving soil to the body, taking the feeling of the cycles of nature, comprehend them and reconnect. Then, it will be possible to carry out expressing exercises to heal and improve health.

Expressing through shaking, expressing through unloading, expressing through breathing exercises; it relaxes the mind, and also the body, it stops inertia, it gives us the time to do each thing, to be present in every situation, to autosuggest positively, installing reproductive affirmations; all these can help us feel well with ourselves, express and building our health.

23. DARK ILLUSIONS

This is one of the mental motives that generates most dissatisfaction, and as a direct consequence it brings more suffering, those are the expectations and the confusion of what's real from what's imaginary.

If the ego identifies with the expectation and projects it, and then things don't go as we have imagined them to be, the mind will generate dissatisfaction and it will be deposited in our subconscious, provoking psychological, emotional and physical instability, affecting the functioning of the apparatus in which we live through, and it will be able to create suffering. If the ego gets misidentified from expectation, it will not project it to the world, the mind won't measure events according to these and it will accept things as they are.

The unexpected will always come along, what's expected won't necessarily come.

A family goes on vacation for a week to Hawaii. They arrive to the hotel and in the prior instant to head to the beach, a strong storm begins. Hours pass and the storm keeps going. Then they stay at the hotel for the day. The next day, when they wake up, they discover that the storm is still present. The day passes and they lay down. The next day, when they wake up, they discover that the storm is still present. And so on, for each one of the days of their vacation. Until the last day, when they are going to the airport to take the plane back, the storm stops and the sun is visible again.

There are those who have a bad time if placed on that situation. Why is that? What is the problem with the rain? Rain is beautiful, it is useful, it is necessary for life on this planet and it does well. However, there are those who are capable to get angry at rain. They can even take things personally and get angry at nature, believing that it is acting against them, that if it rained it was something that the world did against them. Something simple happened in this story: they had installed a picture in their minds, they pictured themselves laying down in the sun, the white sand before them, the light blue sky above them, the coconut with a straw on their hands; the post card of their vacations in Hawaii. They had settled a picture about their expectations and imagined that was how their vacations would turn out, they projected this imagination and believed it so badly that they took it as their reality. Then they arrived to Hawaii, they found out that what was happening had nothing to do with what they have imagined and judged reality with their imagination, they measured what happened according to what they imagined that would had happened. The contrast in which they were is huge, reality doesn't adjust to the mold of imagination. Because of that they get frustrated, installing dissatisfaction, getting distressed and they are capable of creating suffering from that.

If reality sometimes concurs with what you have imagined that would happen, it will only be by chance. We don't control humanity, the planet and the universe, we don't have the capability to make things happen exactly as expected.

An uncontrolled mind will mix everything up; it will confuse what has been imagined with reality and judge reality according to imagination. Then, it would seek to force the world to adequate to its mental mold, it will force others to adequate according to its expectations, it will try to adapt reality to imagination, and won't know how to enjoy things simply as they are. It rains on vacation. Wonderful. There are many things that can be done while it is raining. The uncontrolled mind will confuse imagination with reality on every circumstance; at work, in relationships, with their development, with the world, and with its world. It will expect that the evolution of its labor will go as it imagined, that its partner behaves as it desires, that its friend behave as it hankers to, that the world will behave as it expects. It will hold to these expectations and then it will be frustrated when it discovers that its work or job has not evolved as imagined, that its partner has not done what it desired, that its friend has not behaved as it wanted, that the world didn't do what it said. We don't expect that our work will fail, that our partner may leave us, that our friend may change, that the world don't do what we wanted. Things can happen differently from what we imagined. In fact, it is a rule: it will be different from what you imagined. If we hold to expectations we will get frustrated, install dissatisfaction and generate suffering. An uncontrolled mind will judge the present according to imagination, and with that, it will measure its level of success or failure: «The present was better than what was imagined... ¡What a success!», «The present was worse than what was imagined... ¡What a failure!».

We tend to expect that the world will behave as we imagined. Then we measure success and failure based on the level of misalignment of reality according to imagination. It will not happen as expected, it is not under our control; many forces have interacted so each thing happened as it happened. To make things happen exactly as we imagined and expect that we would have a level of holly awareness, so it will manifest into the others' body.

If we hold to expectation, and the unexpected happens, dissatisfaction appears. Automatically, negative energy gets accumulated. If you expect one thing and the other happens: instant dissatisfaction. Check the amount of expectations that you deposit on daily basis, on your friends, children, family, couple, parents, people on the street, work, and so on. Then, observe how many of these expectations transform into dissatisfaction.

Educating the mind helps us not to create these kinds of tensions inside of us. Not to deposit imaginary absurd toward an uncertain future. And in case we do it, we should know how to make a difference between imagination and reality.

It is not the same to define objectives -which is what a trained mind does- than imagining madly, depositing expectations, holding to them and confusing reality with imagination. You can define objectives and turn back your sight to the present, working on each one of the steps, accepting things to happen as they do and actuating in present according to what you consider more convenient, or how you feel it. If you are here, in the present, seeing things as they happen, you can actuate with the world, offering it the best of you on every instant. If we keep holding to projections and expectations, we will live ephemeral happiness and extraordinary sadness, ephemeral success and fantastic failure, according to how reality shows, regarding what was imagined. We would live with the contrast between reality and imagination with tremendous passion, going from a state to another, from expectation to expectation, measuring the world according to fantasy.

A mind that gets trained, an essential being that gives space to the mind and de-identifies the ego from imagination and expectation, it will take things as they are, it will know what is happening, whatever it is, it is real; and what we imagine will be used to define objectives, directions or installing alternatives. We would live from present to present, aware on each moment, through full acceptance. We would behave according to what happens, and what is imagined won't transform into a problem or motive for suffering.

Things are as they are, the world is as it is. The best we can do on every moment is to be on each moment. The best we can do for ourselves is being with ourselves. When we are self aware we are aware of everything.

An uncontrolled mind will be far from what is really happening; but instead of playing with the world, accepting things as they are and giving the best on each moment, it supposes. It digs mentally, scratches mad intellectual theories, it believes them, take them as truth, and then behaves according to this. It proposes things and believes them. Takes it and judges others, its work, its job and the world according to this. It follows what logic and reason say; without observing all the perspectives, and only seeing a small angle of the truth, and that each one can find their own reasons to believe that it is logical, that it is true, that it is that way. It acts by supposing. As a result from digging and speculating, it acts based on mad ideas, that have nothing to do with what happens in its entirety. Afterwards, according to the result of its actions and what happens, it allocates the responsibility to luck. The mind takes these mad ideas, believes them, thinks they are right and explains the result with fate.

This delirious situation can be seen from the outside. However, when we are inside of it, we believe that our truth is the truth, we believe that our interpretation is the world's interpretation. When we take distance and observe as a silent witness, we can discover that everything is not as it looks. If we observe like a silent witness we will see what is behind of everything and say: «this is madness!». But when we are in the inside, this small logic starts to make sense. When we observe from the outside, we can discover that we are not seeing the other's reality, that not everything that the mind tells us is right, the mind is not always right and it is not necessarily useful to act according to reason and that it is not necessarily useful to act according to the suppositions of an uncontrolled mind.

Check how many times a day you act based on suppositions instead of acting according to what the situation requires. How many times a day do we adjudge the results of events to fate or to luck.

Maybe any of this has anything to do with luck, maybe fate is not acting that way, maybe it is not about the uncontrolled mind being right or not, or if the scientific mind that analyses a small event without seeing the whole, finds what is happening logical or not. Maybe the mind is not always right. Maybe, the world works beyond what we can see, and not everything is reasonable or logical, and not everything is how we imagine or suppose it to be. Maybe, giving space and flexibility to the mind, absorbing other points of view and stopping judging, accepting things as they are and stopping supposing, not taking everything personally and stopping to identify with everything that happens, might result useful to move forward and stop crashing.

The mind finds reasons to justify any opinion. If we persist in ways of acting of agitation and dispersion, we would spend time supposing, imagining, depositing expectations, suspecting, creating fabulous stories that cover uncertainty with fantastic theories, identifying with those thoughts and acting motivated by them.

We can try to find any circumstance that we have defined in some way, that you think it is that way, that you have analyzed using logic and that you concluded something about. Once you find this circumstance, you can try to find different points of view to it; seeing it in other ways. We can see it in as many ways as we dare to (by accessing to the unstable mind). Once you have done this exercise, you can dear to stop judging the situation, allowing the mystery to act without knowing how it works, quit acting by logical analysis and reason, to allow the entrance of intuition and emotion. We should stop filling the uncertain with theories, and allow the unknown and uncertainty to talk.

24. EVERYTHING IS PERSONAL, AND NOT THAT MUCH

Attachment comes as the result of a mind acting without control, that identifies rigidly with an idea, it solidifies it and makes itself a slave of it. This mind will hold to situations and won't allow itself to let them go, making its becoming a constant chaos, dragging the past without allowing itself to see the present, annulling its capacity of discernment, creating guilt, resentment, obsessions, exaggerated passions, installing negative emotions into the environment, hurting itself and hurting others. This attachment works with repetitive thoughts, installing restrictive ideas and creating blocks on every level: psychological, emotional, sexual, physical, astral and mental. Attachment blocks the flow of life and kills. Makes us carry the weight of useless things and makes us spend time feeding them; it increases the weight of what we are carrying and entertains us to keep making it grow. Attachment hinders and affects the free living.

In order to move apart from attachment, and even avoiding to create it, it is necessary that the mind lives the present, that it works in the ways of acting of concentration and mental annihilation, as we also train the unstable mind, the intellect, the subconscious and the ego. If we are already attached to something, first it will be necessary to recognize it, and once we have done the recognition, cultivate sacred indifference. Sacred indifference will be the result of giving space to the mind, to de-identify the ego from attachment, setting useful objectives and focusing on taking directions and organizing. When we focus our mind in what's useful, as a counterpart, it will stop focusing on the useless; it will cultivate the sacred indifference, which will make emotions regarding to it deflate, it will also deflate attachment itself.

Then, once the mind is free from attachment, it will be useful to go back to the shadow to investigate what was the reason that caused it, what memory is saved in the subconscious that was trying to get out to find light and being recognized. Because if there is attachment, and we had the capability to escape from ourselves and focusing on something external, identifying with it and creating a great problem, it is because there was something right there (not in the object of desire, but in the desire itself).

25. DON´T WORRY, BE HAPPY

The story tells that there were two friends arguing about their respective perspectives of the world. One saw the world as a wide, fresh, bright and subtle space; the other, saw it as a closed, heavy, dark and dense place. They were on the street arguing and shouting; each one of them made a huge list of arguments in favor of their perspectives and each argument sounded valid.

The discussion stopped at the moment when a child passed by them and heard them arguing. The kid told them that each one spoke as their body was: the one that saw the world as a wide, fresh, bright and subtle place, placed the head looking toward the sky while talking; while the one that the one that considered the world a closed, heavy, dark and dense place, lowered the sight to the ground while discoursing. Both became silent against the words of the child. Then, the child continued: telling that both of them were right, but their truth wasn't absolute, that each one perceived a part of the whole.

Both of them remained silent a bit longer and then told the child to go away, that they were having an adult conversation, and they continued to discuss.

We shouldn't overlook things, while we work with the mind and train it to make it a great tool, while we get inside of its darkness to recognize what we are not recognizing, while we separate from it to be a silent witness that controls it, and develop our powers; it is also useful to incorporate the bright side.

We have the capability to voluntarily choose which polarity we are gonna give to each one of our thoughts. We can choose them, with the intellect, whether we see situations as positive, negative or neutral. While the work of the middle track is a source of knowledge -neutral sight-, the positive perspective will bring us joy and make the journey more entertaining. If we can choose how we are going to see each instant, if we can find infinite points of view toward the same point, it will be useful to install the bright side as the option we can appeal to each time we want to be joyful. In fact, it is the polarity that love presents, the one that allow us to transgress, expand, grow and evolve. If everything isn't good or bad, but everything is as it is, we can take things for our own good. Whatever it is. If our thoughts, words and actions create a network of causality and reactions in the universe that determine our becoming, we can propose things that will make us and the world well. If we can play to put this mental flexibility and try different points of view, then we can choose consciously a point of view that makes us and others well. Something that has to do with being glad on every situation. It is possible, on every situation.

If things are not absolute, with a connotation, but they can be positive, negative or neutral, we can choose consciously which polarity we are going to charge it with. If we can do it, we can find the bright side of everything. It is all about getting away from the only and rigid point of view, so we see other options, finding the bright side.

This might lead us to positive self-suggestion: affirmations that make us well. If the universe hears everything we say, think and do, then we can use it on our favor and send things that are useful to us. We can get up and decide something nice; we would start the day with a smile; we can set affirmations on paper and put it in our pockets, folders, wallet, vehicle, house, furniture. We prepare an authorization and suggestion: «I am capable, I am worthy, I authorize myself». When we make decisions, we will connect to the bright side of every decision. When we work, we will connect with the dignity of acting. When we dialog, we will connect with the dignity of sharing. When we eat, we will connect with the beauty of the food and the sacred ritual that matters is offering to hold it. Digest, touch your stomach and bless the process that the great laboratory holds. When the night falls, take a shower, look at yourself in the mirror, naked, and reconnect to your body. Make a balance of what you have lived during the day, and seek for the bright side of each circumstance. Self-observe and, also, evaluate and work with yourself, finish the balance with a positive aspect. Lay down and bless the bed and the sleep.

Try to use the power of the mind to improve, pick voluntarily what make us well and enjoy our going through the world. This activity sets us in a positive frequency, it adds constructive ideas, expand the mind, help us to be more self-aware and heals the body.

We can take the «Things happen for a reason» mental attitude, looking for the best on each circumstance, while we function positively. We can see all this for our good, we can consciously find joy, discover reasons to be satisfied with everything that is happening, appreciating life, our life, other's life, reconnecting with the dignity of being alive.

CHAPTER NINE
FURTHER FROM THE MIND

1. EVERYTHING HAPPENS FOR A REASON

2. EVERYTHING PASSES

3. TRUTH OR LIE?

4. PUPPETS OF A HOLY DANCE

5. MAKING POSSIBLE THE IMPOSSIBLE

6. MASTERS OF FATE

7. KNOW YOURSELF

1. EVERYTHING HAPPENS FOR A REASON

Everything happens for a reason. That reason might be the encounter of everything that happened before, with the present, in addition with what the mystery dictates. Either way, let it be what it is. Instead of defining and interpreting by giving it names, it is useful to be a silent witness of events, without making any judgment about it.

If there is a moment in which I dare to balance everything that has happened, it would be the last annihilation of air prior to the arrival of death. Even so, I doubt I dare to make that judgment in that moment; because even then, uncertainty would be present, the unknown and the mystery that acts. I don't know what is coming up next; therefore, neither can I know exactly why happened what happened. It is for a reason, everything happens for a reason, and it will happen for something.

The uncontrolled mind will be defining the world and defining the essential being; it will be naming events such as «good», «bad», «success», «failure», «good luck», «bad luck», «tragedies», and so on. These opinions that are in favor or against things are not useful, they are not reproductive, and they don't contribute to anything.

There isa superior intelligence that is working through us. The mind can't reach everything; the thought dissolves in the present, the mind doesn't know how to act toward mystery, the infinite and the unknown. It is useful to give part of the advance to mystery, and trying not to explain everything, or looking for a reason for everything. There are zones that the mind can't reach; zones that can surpass what the mind sees as insuperable, zones that can see the exit when the mind can't. They key on this work is not to despair. Because while life goes on, we are full of possibilities. Don't despair. Because whatever it is, everything passes.

There are spirits queuing for thousands of millions of years, waiting their turn to incarnate. Being alive is a divine miracle, is an unmatched luck, a right, a precious merit.

We can also see this from the scientific point of view: an average ejaculation contains three hundred million sperms; the average probability to win the lotto is one in five millions; so, we are more likely to win the lotto fifty nine times in a row than being born once.

Living is a divine miracle, it is a great chance, it's something wonderful, and if we are here it is because we can, and we deserve to be here. If we are alive, it is because we have the capability to live fully, evolve, develop, change, grow, and experience a healthy life, with happiness and joy.

2. EVERYTHING PASSES

I will tell you something that destroys constructions, relieves hearts, abandon excitement and frees us from tragedy: everything passes. It is an innate condition of manifestation. Everything that happens is temporary, everything there is, is ephemeral, what remain is our essential being, that lives through our body and is beyond from subtle matter and dense matter. Everything passes. When the exit can't be seen it is useful to remember it: everything passes. When we are stuck in suffering and we don't know how to work upon it, everything passes. When you discover injustice and the world seems impossible, everything passes. When life presents adversity and challenges, everything passes.

There are people that know how to survive failure, but then, they don't know how to survive success. Because they get stuck to the past situation, attached wildly, without accepting that even that is going to pass. Everything we see is impermanent. If it is manifested, we can't remain forever, because everything that is ever born dies. If we are here, whatever it is, if we are born somehow, it will happen in some other way. Problems pass, tragedies pass, success pass, emotions pass, failure passes, relationships pass, life itself passes. Life flows, it is permanently dynamic, in constant change between its beginning (birth) and its end (death). And this beginning and this end are bridges that work between the unknown and life (birth) and between life and the unknown (death). In the middle, life is in constant transformation. Everything passes. Everything changes. Nothing remains.

3. TRUTH OR LIE?

We don't know for sure what is real and what is not, if everything is a lie or not. We know that if it is manifested, it meets the three phases of the manifestation: creation, maintenance and destruction. From cells to galaxies. We perceive through our mind and live through the mental projection. Then everything could be interpreted as illusions. However, when we are slammed, it hurts. We have the capability to feel; what creates doubt about the dream and makes it more vivid. Something is happening. Something bigger than ourselves is experiencing us. Meanwhile, we are equipped with the capability of thinking, feeling, needing, wishing and also educating our minds, so we can be better at coping with our becoming. If we call the permanent a truth and the impermanent a lie, then everything would be a lie. If reality is eternal, absolute, infinite and total, then all these would be and ephemeral extension of that reality.

4. PUPPETS OF A HOLY DANCE

We believe we can control a lot of things, and maybe it is not much that we can domain. If we are doing a great job at mental training, we can deal with the soul's clothing, choosing exactly what we think, say and do. And that will change the experience we get in this life categorically. Nevertheless, and still, that is a tiny part of everything that is happening. The mystery is working through all of us and is taking care of almost everything. This superior intelligence that crosses us, controls most of the things that happen. If we observe the performance of your body, sexuality, emotions, mind, the world, the planet, galaxies and the universe, we can se that there is something greater that is doing all the work for us. We don't know how it is doing it, neither why it is doing it, nor what it is doing it for, but it is doing it. Life is happening. What we can do, while it happens, is to give the best of us. Working to know ourselves, discover ourselves and tame our powers. However, and still, there will be a sacred mechanism taking care of most of the things that involve us.

A man is driving his car on the road. Suddenly, he is surprised when he discovers that sometimes when he turns right, the car turns left. Some other times he turns left and the car goes right. Sometimes, the vehicle obeys, some others, not so much. Suddenly, he tries to breuk and the car accelerates. Then, he tries to accelerate and the car stops. He looks back and to the sides, and he sees a lot of people in the same situation as his in their vehicles; some of them have worried faces, some others are yelling and throwing a tantrum, some others are crying, others asking for help. Then, it occurs to him to look down and he discovers that each one of the cars are on a truck that transports vehicles.

Maybe, we go through life somewhat like that, believing that we control a lot while we don't control so much. It is very little what is under our control, and if we can control that little part, we can enjoy the ride.

It would be useful to quit resistance while we do this work, abandoning the psychological and emotional blocking, and surrender to the divine. Surrender to what we can't resolve, to what worries us, to what we don't understand, to what affects us, to what we have and don't want, to what we expect, to what distresses us, to what frustrates us, to what disconcerts us, to what despairs us. Surrendering completely and stopping to carry the responsibility of absolutely everything that happen to us.

5. MAKING POSSIBLE THE IMPOSSIBLE

If there is something that you believe you can accomplish, observe it again. There are a few things we can't do and there are many excuses that we use not to do them.

Our essence, that has been manifested, includes everything that is revealed. Therefore, we are the manifestation of infinite possibilities. Of course, when we are born we take a body and a shape, we follow certain laws, and we come with certain conditions. However, our root is the infinite. The whole potency is within us.

Saying this implies that right now, if you go to the window, you can fly away. There are certain rules that we meet while we manifest them on a global level and project them among everyone else with our mind. However, we can do a great part of the things that we think we are not capable of. A big part of what you think is impossible, is possible. Everything that is possible started being impossible and everything that is difficult stops being hard when it gets done. If you observe the elements that surround you on this very moment, you will discover a great number of inventions that, if we mention them to people from five thousand years ago, they wouldn't believe us. We are surrounded by what once was seen as impossible. Imagine that you tell someone from five thousand years ago about paper, pencils, bikes, computers, phones, smartphones and so on. They would see us like sorcerers, wizards or aliens. Everything that now seems obvious, wasn't that way once. Everything that now seems impossible to you, will be possible once it gets done.

While we are alive, we are full potency, every possibility of change and action. Everything that seems impossible becomes possible if it gets done. When we imagine it, we start creating it. This great power is within us and allows us to access to the infinite possibilities -through the unstable mind- to give them motion – through the intellect's decision – and executing things that can be innocently believed as impossible – through a restrictive idea settled in the subconscious and the ego that is identified with it -. Only because we don't see it doesn't mean that it doesn't exist. Our vision is capable of restricting the possibilities, but life itself is not limited.

6. MASTERS OF FATE

While we give the best of ourselves at every instant, there are unavoidable things. The future, the unknown, the uncertain will tell us what the mystery should tell us. The unavoidable acts as the weight of the present that gets installed within us and offers us what the world has to give us. While we execute our actions, we keep standing on the world. Even if we live under different dimensions simultaneously, when we are awaken, we are here, and when we are asleep, we are elsewhere without loosing this one. While we take our lives, life is taking us with it. While we control our actions, the universe's actions cannot be controlled. The world is how it is. The visible face we perceive; the invisible face is what we discover if we dare to. Fighting against ourselves won't make us enjoy it. Trusting the natural process becomes blessing and joyful, while we experience our journey through this world. Things are how they are, a tree is a tree, the air is the air. The world is the world. The stars are stars. By accepting ourselves, we accept the world.

7. KNOW YOURSELF

«Defining with words the answer to the question of 'who am I?' is impossible. The closest to do it, is saying, Sat-Chit-Ananda, three words from sanskrit that mean "being-said awareness". Beyond everything that isn't, we can find what it is, the true self. Beyond every illusion, awareness is found. Beyond any suffering, joy is found. Being the existence, the knowledge, and the blessing.»[8]

We don't even know who we are. If we put definitions we create toward ourselves aside, if we work on every part of the mind and its ways of acting, what remains becomes indefinable. We can get close, saying that everything we are exists, what we are has the capability to be self-aware and what we are is covered with joy. This can get us very close to our true name; even so, the name itself becomes unpronounceable.

---

[8] Leandro Taub, Holy Devil

CHAPTER 10

GIVING IN

1. BETWEEN HEAVEN AND HELL

2. THE POWER OF LIES

3. THERE IS NOTHING BUT YOU

4. WHAT YOU FEAR HIDES WHAT YOU DESIRE

1. BETWEEN HEAVEN AND HELL

The disciple reached his master and asked him to tell him what was the difference between heaven and hell. The master answered.

— In hell, I see big mountains, in the middle of those mountains a see a great forest, in the middle of the forest I see a great meadow, in the middle of the meadow I see a big bowl with a mountain of rice, surrounding that bowl there are millions of people with five meter chopsticks trying to eat the rice, but they can't because the length of the chopsticks doesn't allow them to put the rice in their mouths.

— In heaven, I see big mountains, in the middle of those mountains a see a great forest, in the middle of the forest I see a great meadow, in the middle of the meadow I see a big bowl with a mountain of rice, surrounding that bowl there are millions of people with five meter chopsticks trying to eat one another.

What we can do for ourselves is what we do for the world. What we do for the world is what we do for ourselves. One can't be without the other.

2. THE POWER OF LIES

There are two kinds of terminal patients laying on hospital beds. One of them has the bed next to the window and the other next to the hallway door. The one with the bed next to the window, talks to the next patient about the adventures of what can be seen from there; giving details about the landscape that can be seen from distance, the city in full motion, buildings and their colors, the graffiti that some youngsters make on a wall from far away, the way in which the vehicles are parked in the parking lot, the changing rhythm of the traffic lights on avenues that seems like a Beethoven melody, the way that people walk on the sidewalks and all the stories that can be seen daily. Until death comes one day.

A few days after death, the patient that had the bed next to the door asks the nurses to put him on the bed next to the window, because he would like to see the landscape and keep enjoying the adventures that his companion talked about. The nurses do what the patient asks. When he gets to the new bed, he discovers that the window's view collides with a wall of the building.

Only because everything is that way, doesn't mean we should read it that way. We will live what we project and according to how we project it and how we take that projection. There are useful lies, that cheer our lives up. Maybe it wasn't the wall what the patient was talking about from the bed, but his tale was useful. There are true emotions over fake events, and if the emotion is genuine, the truth about the fact that produces it stops to matter, it is already incorporated as a vital experience. This doesn't mean that if you feel in some way, the world would feel the same, but if I feel it that way, my world would be that way. We don't know yet what is real and what isn't, what we know is what we could understand and feel. That made our experience vital. And even if it is ephemeral, if it passes, and leaves no trace, it was worth the adventure. Maybe life has only one meaning and it is not as chaotic as it seems; living longer, in better conditions, evolving, reproducing, and fundamentally enjoying the ride while we live, we will discover the life's meaning. It is useful to ask ourselves if what we are doing goes with the meaning of life, and if there is any sign, we should dare to follow it. Everything is and becomes sacred on the road.

3. THERE IS NOTHING BUT YOU

They can tell you what they have done and what they haven't. However, others' path will never be your path. What we can do is to tell their experiences, the little they could gather from those words about them. Each one makes their own path. Your best master will be your last master, because it will take you to the limit of disappearing, so you become your own guide. Why does it matter what they can tell? If you take this strongly, you will get disappointed with me, because I will come in a while to propose something new or because you advance beyond this. While we discover ourselves, while we reveal who we are, the adventure keeps going. If you tell a secret, the magic trick looses its grace. If you tell the end of a story, the adventure looses its charm. It is not about being taken by the hand and get everything figured out. It is not about getting your food chewed and given with a spoon. While we discover ourselves, each one of us makes their own path. And while we discover ourselves, it is useful not to despair. Being found here, experiencing life, with the capacity to discover ourselves, it is a divine miracle.

A man in a fair sees a magician doing tricks of miraculous magic. After the show the man reached the magician and asked how he did all those magic tricks that look like miracles. The magician answered that there is no trick, they are simply miracles.

—*Who do you think you are? Is it that you believe you are god and you can do mira-*

cles? —Says the man to the magician

—Yes —answers the magician.

— If you are god, then I'm god too — yells the man angrily

—Quite so… —answers the magician—, the difference is that I know it and you don't.

4. WHAT YOU FEAR HIDES WHAT YOU DESIRE

The story tells that a very wealthy man, in his last time of life, decided to give away and spend all the money he had. One day, one of his friends reached him and asked him why he was doing that, and if he didn't care about his offspring. The man answered yes, that it was for them that he would spend all of his money before dying.

In the life we experience between birth and death, we have been offered two powerful and useful tools: love and fear. Fear is there, not only to help us to protect, to gestate, to establish ourselves and to balance, but also to indicate what we desire. Once our desire is recognized, we can access to another useful tool, that will potentiate us and help us to dare to achieve it, love.

— HOW DID YOU DO WHAT WAS IMPOSSIBLE TO DO?

— I DIDN'T KNOW IT WAS IMPOSSIBLE

If you are willing, please write your Book Review

in Amazon and Goodreads.

For more information, you can follow the author Leandro Taub,

on his website and social media:

www.leandrotaub.com

@LeandroTaub

Made in the USA
Middletown, DE
14 March 2023